D0585284

COLLEGE LIBRARY

4491

COACHING CRICKET

COACHING CRICKET

Keith Andrew

Director of Coaching
National Cricket Association

THE CROWOOD PRESS

First published in 1986 by
THE CROWOOD PRESS
Ramsbury, Marlborough
Wiltshire SN8 2HE

© Keith Andrew 1986

All rights reserved. No part of this publication may be reproduced or
transmitted in any form or by any means, electronic or mechanical,
including photocopy, recording, or any information storage and
retrieval system without permission in writing from the publishers.

British Library Cataloguing in Publication Data

Andrew, Keith
    Coaching cricket.
    1.   Cricket coaching
    I.   Title
    769.35'8'077   GV 926
    ISBN 0-946284-13-X

Acknowledgements

MCC and NCA for permission to use excerpts from *The MCC Coaching Book*
and *Test Cricket in Clubs and Schools*.

The National Coaching Foundation for the use of coaching caricatures
on which Figs 2 and 72 are based.

Test match photographs by Patrick Eagar
Coaching photographs by author
Cover photographs by Patrick Eagar
Line illustrations by Annette Findlay

Typeset by Alacrity Phototypesetters,
Banwell Castle, Weston-super-Mare.
Printed in Great Britain.

Contents

Keith Andrew is a qualified schoolteacher and former lecturer at the Northampton College of Technology. He joined Northamptonshire CCC in 1953 and during a distinguished career he established a number of wicket-keeping records. He represented England against Australia and the West Indies, and in 1962 became one of the youngest professional captains in cricket history, leading his county through five very successful years. In 1975 Keith joined the National Cricket Association, and has been Director of Coaching since 1979. He is the author of the bestselling book, *The Skills of Cricket*, published by Crowood in 1984.

No matter at what level of cricket coaching you are involved, there is something in this book for you. Never before has the range of information on the techniques of coaching cricket as a skill in its own right been dealt with so comprehensively.

I am one of the lucky cricketers, having been guided through my early years in the game by men of commitment and knowledge. I think the type of men who encouraged me will find this book stimulating and challenging.

Mike Gatting
England and Middlesex CCC

This book complements Keith's previous book *The Skills of Cricket* and is ideal for anyone with an interest in coaching or teaching cricket, whether he be an expert or a beginner.

I am sure that *Coaching Cricket* will be an asset to the game that brings so much to our way of life.

J.D. Robson
Chairman, National Cricket Association

Introduction

Whilst coaching cricket is a profession for some and a hobby for others, when entered into in the right spirit it has much to offer everyone involved. It brings together kindred spirits with a common desire to be a part of a way of life. It touches many people, giving feeling, expression and enjoyment to young and old alike. For those who are involved in maintaining cricket's traditions and values and passing them on to our young people, there can be nothing but the deepest pride and satisfaction.

Whether you are a paying spectator, a club member, a former player, a committee member or simply an involved schoolteacher or parent, you will probably be a coach of sorts. At least you will have an opinion about the way the game is played, and the ability of certain players. You will almost certainly query why the captain did this, when he should have done that ... and why not indeed? Isn't that what participation is all about and why sport is such an integral part of society? If you are a player, particularly a well-known player, do not underestimate your influence as a coach, whether you profess to be one or not. Young enthusiasts will copy your style and play Test matches where the sun always shines and they, with their heroes, always win. Whilst life isn't like that and this book is hopefully a down-to-earth, technical but practical treatise on coaching cricket, our dreams must always be our own and worthy of preserving and sometimes recreating.

You may already be involved in coaching or perhaps you enjoy the thought of training young cricketers and putting something back into the game; whichever, please read on as it is said that the first few minutes of any relationship are vital. Whether yours turns out to be a mild flirtation or a lifelong passion, cricket and coaching will welcome you with open arms and in return will surely add a special bonus to your interest in sport and life in general.

Now to the subject in a little more depth. You may already have noticed my use of the word 'training' as against 'coaching'. This is not intended to further confuse the already confused interpretations of both words – it is simply a means of highlighting the need to differentiate between them from the beginning. For the record, this book is concerned with the overall training of coaches and is both a sequel and a complement to my earlier book *The Skills of Cricket*, which is, by definition, concerned with the coaching of players. In other words, from the point of view of my writings coaching is a specific aspect of training, which indicates that training is the more complete and yet general definition of the coach's work!

As far as cricket is concerned, in my opinion, if athletes can be either trained or coached to lift heavier weights, jump higher, run faster, throw further or whatever, surely cricketers can be similarly trained or coached to bowl faster, hit the ball harder and probably more accurately

1

and consequently be more effective players than they might otherwise have been. There is no reason why flair should go out of the window, just because realism comes in, as come it must if progress is to be made and cricket is to compete with other sports in the future. Please do not say 'cricket is different'!

In the context of this dialogue it is perhaps important to mention other words that may well be combined for improving a player's performance. The words I am thinking of are *art* and *science*. Cricket of all games, in its hundreds of years of history and because of its very nature, has been associated with great artists, if not so many scientists. Naturally, art is to do with talent or vice versa and it may be said that cricket without art is not cricket and I, for one, believe this to be true. However, in a similar vein I may go on and suggest that an injection of science may not go amiss in benefiting the game, if accomplished with a care and compassion for it. For those whose weekly visit to the crease hardly ever results in double figures, what a thrill it must be when through some small improvement in technique, those scores of 'five' become 'fifteens' and sometimes 'fifties'. Can scoring a hundred in a Test match be a greater thrill than scoring your first fifty for your school, or club, when never before have you reached ten? I do not know, but if science can produce either, who can argue against it? Alternatively if science can combine with art and produce fast bowlers to rival the greatest would anyone quibble? I think not!

Finally let me raise one other factor that must concern us all in cricket. By all means let coaches work hard and develop the skills and techniques of our young players to perform on the field, to the very best of their ability. But let us *all* in cricket take a share in the development of other attributes – call it personality, character, charisma if you like; but whatever we call it, let it be worthy of the game.

It is most unlikely that this and my previous book *The Skills of Cricket* would have been written if I had not at some stage in recent years been influenced by a number of cricketing people and coaches in particular. Let me give the greatest credit to my colleagues over these years, the six NCA Regional National Coaches: Bob Carter, Bob Cottam, Doug Ferguson, Les Lenham, Graham Saville and David Wilson. I should like to think that a good slice of their collective technical expertise has rubbed off and shows in my writings. The two Dons, Bennett and Wilson, Chief Coaches of Middlesex and MCC are also valuable allies in my endeavours. My life-long friend in Australia, Frank Tyson, has set the highest standards in cricket coaching literature and in doing so has stimulated my interest and efforts. There are many others. I think particularly of Gubby Allen, Freddie Brown, Don Robson and the late Jim Lane, but it is being a part of the National Cricket Association that is perhaps the real catalyst for me. I am grateful.

Keith Andrew

My Team Worth Watching

Most cricket lovers will argue for hours over their 'best' team, whether it be since the war, before the war, of all time, and so on. The chapters of this book have given me the opportunity of selecting a team of current Test players that I should most like to watch winning. One photograph is shown at the beginning of each chapter. In batting order they are:

Sunil Gavaskar (India)
A magnificent player of fast bowling with a temperament to play the bowling on its merits and make big scores.

Gordon Greenidge (West Indies)
A brilliant and powerful stroke player who will destroy anything but the best attack.

David Gower (England)
David has a marvellous record. This team is selected not only for its potential to win matches but for the virtuosity of its players.

Vivian Richards (West Indies)
Viv must surely be one of the all time great batsmen. He personifies the spirit of all the great West Indian batsmen with the complete freedom and quality of his stroke play.

Allan Border (Australia)
If for some reason things had gone wrong and my team was in trouble, who else but Allan Border would anyone wish to see coming to the wicket.

Ian Botham (England)
In this batting side, what might happen when Ian comes to the wicket I just cannot imagine. Do not forget he is our third pace bowler with over 300 Test wickets.

Jeffrey Dujon (West Indies)
Keeping wicket magnificently to the world's fastest attack is giving Jeffrey a cricketer's biggest fillip – confidence. I am sure he would prove capable of coping with the wiles of Abdul Qadir and the subtlety of John Emburey – and what a magnificent batsman!

Richard Hadlee (New Zealand)
Ranked alongside Malcolm Marshall as one of the great fast bowlers, if there is a little moisture around or if the atmosphere will help the ball swing, Richard might even be slightly ahead of Malcolm.

Malcolm Marshall (West Indies)
Malcolm is without question one of the greatest fast bowlers of all time – strong, hostile, accurate and as fast as they come. Not only that, he can bat and field as well.

John Emburey (England)
In my book a balanced side, capable of bowling at least eighteen overs an hour, will need the world's best finger spinner. If the wicket takes spin, John could be the match winner.

Abdul Qadir (Pakistan)
Abdul, perhaps the only world class leg spin bowler, will be a force on any wicket, but with a little bounce and turn only the very best batsmen will cope with him.

Fig 1 Sunil Gavaskar (India)

1 The Role of the Coach

I am sure that in the training of any cricketer, it is fair to say that the cricket coach can, and maybe should, play the most significant role. Having said this, the problem is to identify firstly the coach and secondly what he may aspire to in the overall training of an individual, a team, or both.

There are, of course, any number of opinions as to how coaches may be described and what their position is in the cricket scene. The Oxford Dictionary describes a coach as a 'tutor or trainer of competitors for examination or athletic contest', which from most people's point of view leaves a lot to the imagination.

ATTRIBUTES REQUIRED

Let us look at the attributes one might hope for, to some degree or other, in our complete cricket coach.

The Complete Cricket Coach

1. Has a good knowledge of all the recognised skills and techniques of coaching.
2. Has an equally sound knowledge of all the skills and techniques of playing cricket.
3. Will be capable preferably of demonstrating, or arranging for the demonstration of, these skills and techniques to a good standard.
4. Will be a teacher in the simplest sense, but with the acquired knowledge of specific teaching methods, required particularly for the teaching of young people. If our coach is a 'teacher', so will he be a historian, with the will to impart a knowledge of, and a feeling for, the history of cricket; something that can only add to a player's all-round personality and value to the game.
5. Will be a motivator, able to activate and inspire a team or an individual.
6. Will be a strong, but not over-strong disciplinarian, able to set high standards in behaviour and appearance and to instil in every player a respect and concern for the game and all those associated with it.
7. Will be a good communicator, verbally, visually and through the written word. The effective passing on of information, not only to players, is greatly underrated by many coaches who are excellent in every other respect.

cont'd

8. Will be a sound administrator; again, sometimes an underrated aspect of the coach's job. The efficient recording of information is more than just useful to the cricket organisations with whom the coach is connected. Proper monitoring of a player's performance and progress can make all the difference to the development of that player.

9. Will be a good manager of people and, like all good managers, our complete coach will be a diplomat, a psychologist and something of a philosopher, with unswerving beliefs in being right about coaching and cricket in general!

10. Will be a leader – not always from the front, but always with the will to initiate development and stimulate progress.

11. He will appreciate that two good demonstrations are worth two thousand words and that too many demonstrations are worth about as much as one bad demonstration.

12. Will be a capable technician; an increasing requirement in our technological age, as sophisticated video and film equipment, not to mention bowling machines and even computers, become an accepted part of the cricket coach's inventory. My coaching nightmare is always the same – an audience of a thousand VIPs, the curtain about to rise on our best coaching film and me with yards of 16mm celluloid tangled around my neck! Don't let it happen to you.

What else must our complete coach be? Certainly a PE Instructor, capable of giving the 'kiss of life' and other forms of resuscitation, if necessary, and, of course, the cricket coach must recognise that all players are different and need specific individual *and* collective attention, in achieving and maintaining maximum fitness for successful playing performance. It does not seem unreasonable either for a coach to take on the role of Public Relations Officer, as coaching, or training in any form for that matter, seems to receive only a minimum of credibility from other sections of the cricket world. A smattering, but not too much, of the lawyer, barrack room or otherwise, may also be an asset, especially when it comes to an argument about the Laws of Cricket, or coaching, or some other equally controversial subject!

Finally, as much as any other single attribute, I can wish on our coaching all-rounder a strong sense of humour, contributing to a warm individual personality that will draw respect from all the players who come under his influence.

Having highlighted the all-round capabilities of our coaching 'genius', let us be more practical and recognise that throughout cricket there is a great need for coaches with just some of the attributes mentioned, in whatever measures they are willing to attain or fortunate enough to be blessed with. Supply and demand are integral aspects of any sport involving the goodwill of voluntary and enthusiastic workers, and more often than not the demand exceeds the supply. Nevertheless, the range of coaching talent is there, at all levels of endeavour. If acknowledged by the coaches themselves, their individual roles can bring them together with a strength and purpose that will lift the game to heights never before achieved and set good examples of cooperation and expertise to people of other walks of life.

What of and what are these individual roles? Where do they fit and are they as compatible as I have suggested? Firstly, consider one side of cricket coaching that can and does take place at the highest levels of player performance. Sometimes, without qualification but with great playing experience, there are those with a strong love of cricket and an innate rapport with the talented young player. Coaches of this ilk are few and far between but, perhaps more than any other group of individuals over the years, have ensured the continuation of cricket and the flowering of its talent. These are the true artists, unsung and sometimes not even remembered, who have been and will continue to be special people in cricket coaching. Have no worries; they will not usurp their role! If anything, they will underrate it and not recognise their real potential, as the sophistication of science takes coaching into another phase in its value to sport.

Already we know of other dedicated coaches of equal value who, purely through enthusiasm and hard work, have acquired coaching skills that give them a

Fig 2

deserved and important place in cricket. Very often without the gift of the born coach, such men and women, purely through their efforts, are also special people and should be recognised as such. It has been my privilege to meet and work with these coaches at both ends of the coaching spectrum and many more, not least the specialists in the coaching of individual skills who have realised that their artistry as players can be enhanced by education and qualification and that coaching is in itself a profession of dignity, with the greatest of rewards.

SUMMARY

I do not suppose that I have defined exactly what the singular role of the coach is, but on reflection I don't suppose I can, as each coach, just like each player, seeks to develop his individual talents. However, I hope I have highlighted the fact that coaching can take many forms and attracts a variety of people with common aims and interests in the game. If this is true, perhaps I can make some further contribution to the title of this chapter by listing important points to remember in the role of any coach.

Key Points

1. Cricket coaching is not an end in itself, but must always be a servant of the game.
2. Silence can be golden: if you have nothing worthwhile to say, say nothing.
3. If you do not enjoy coaching cricketers, do something else.
4. Don't make a crutch of your experience. However, as the saying goes 'I hear and I forget, I see and I remember, *I do and I know!*'
5. Faults are only faults if they inhibit a player from achieving the best possible performance under the prevailing circumstances. Remember also that the manner of achievement is as important as the achievement itself – nearly!
6. Clearly identify the problem before trying to solve it. One might say that cricket bats are designed to score runs, not to play strokes. I say that cricket bats *should* be designed to score runs by playing strokes!
7. Know the Laws of Cricket, as written, and the ethics of cricket, as unwritten. Make sure your players know both at an early age.
8. Dressing-rooms are for players and coaches only.
9. Real talent isn't always obvious. Learn to recognise it when you see it and then nurture it by maintaining a flexible attitude, so that natural flair and individuality are moulded around the basic skills.
10. Optimism, enthusiasm, patience and a sense of humour are a cricket coach's best attributes.
11. Remind your players occasionally that runs cannot be scored or wickets taken in the dressing-room. *cont'd*

12. The best coaches get results quicker by *asking questions*, not giving answers.
13. Coaching the tired player wastes everyone's time.
14. Most cricketers thrive on encouragement.
15. Competition and incentive are just as important in coaching as they are in a match.
16. Good coaches have enquiring minds and acknowledge that they have much to learn.
17. Good coaches – think safety.

In broader terms the role of the cricket coach is to:

* Improve player and team performances.
* Teach all the skills of cricket, as required.
* Maintain the game's traditions and ethics at all costs.
* Promote the game avidly within your sphere of influence.
* Have an open mind and recognise that you can always *improve* your ability as a coach.
* Help other coaches.
* Co-operate with all others who have cricket at heart.

Dangers

No matter how Victorian the comment may sound, there are dangers in coaching – bad coaching that is, but no more than there are dangers in bad teaching, bad building, bad medical care, bad whatever! There are no dangers in good coaching as in everything else that is done well. Good simply means capable, well taught, well qualified, willing to work and experienced as far as possible and so on; but any good coach will be that – or should be.

Fig 3   Gordon Greenidge (West Indies)

2 Group Coaching

Group coaching is simply what it says; coaching in groups, enabling the skills of cricket to be taught, watched and practised by a far greater number of people in a given time than is possible by any other method. A single group is formed by any number over one and as numbers increase so sub-groups can be formed as necessary. Group coaching has a great advantage in that because of its nature it needs to be specific. That is, each skill or part of a skill has to be considered in isolation and its performance and practice pre-arranged. This is an extremely useful and important factor in group coaching, particularly with regard to batting and some aspects of bowling. For example if the pull stroke is to be considered, the ball will need to be bowled or thrown to a defined area on the playing surface for the batsman to play the stroke perfectly; in the case of the pull stroke, a very short ball pitched just outside the leg stump. If the stroke to be considered is the drive, the ball would need to be delivered as a half volley. By following this principle

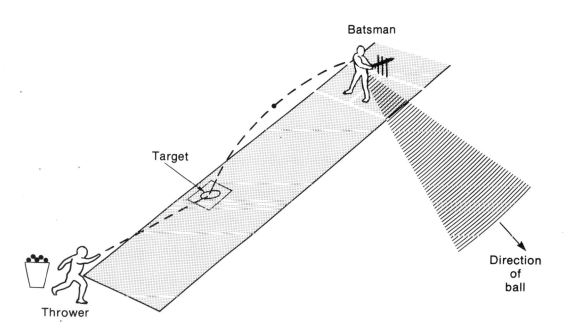

Fig 4   Specific practice of pull stroke.

any particular batting stroke can be performed many times in a given period. This in itself will help the batsman 'groove' the stroke and give him a better chance of reproducing it under pressure in a match. Similarly, bowlers through specific set-ups can achieve skill improvement by controlled repetition of a correct action or part action. Bowling at special targets to suit the different types of bowler is one way of achieving the consistency of length and direction that is so important to the success of a bowler.

Specificity, or put more simply specific set-ups to suit the skill to be coached or taught, is used in other forms of coaching, particularly in skill analysis as applied at high levels of performance. However, as an integral part of group coaching it will perhaps be most appreciated when first teaching young children the basic cricket skills in open spaces without the facility of nets.

ADVANTAGES OF GROUP COACHING

Group coaching:

1. Allows as many players as there is space for, to take part in and benefit from well-organised coaching sessions.
2. Allows the coach to very conveniently use the services and abilities of individuals within the group to perform tasks and set up cricket practices and demonstrations that could not otherwise be achieved.
3. Ensures that the widest range of discussion in question and answer form reaches the ears of those that matter – the young players in the group.

4. Allows the full cycle of activity (bowling, batting and fielding) to be performed and repeated without unnecessary breaks.
5. Produces a competitive element in coaching that is invariably stimulating to the young players.
6. Gives another dimension to a young player's appreciation of what the coach requires. There is nothing like a bad example to highlight a good example, but better still there is nothing like a good example to inspire improvement.

Perhaps above any other comment, it may be said that as a result of group coaching more young players are being properly taught the skills of cricket than ever before. This may not be acknowledged by everyone, but it is none the less irrefutable if one is realistic and accepts the fact that coaching in general is becoming more and more of a skill in its own right – even if it is difficult to define.

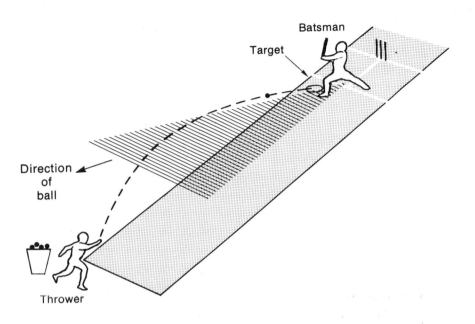

Fig 5   Specific driving practice.

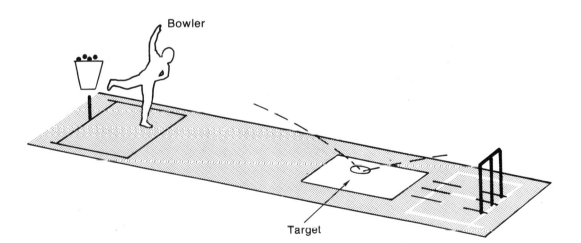

Fig 6   Specific bowling practice.

Fig 7 Group coaching in action.

Fig 8 Batting – the pull stroke. Notice the fielder in position to take the rebound in a narrow space.

Fig 9   Allan Lamb moves into the classic back
        stroke position.

Fig 10   Notice the transfer of weight,
         compared with Fig 8.

METHOD

Having commented generally on the 'whats and whys' of group coaching, we now come to the most important question: how?

BATTING

Let us look firstly at batting. When commencing to teach batting to beginners, the coach should always remember that a good demonstration provides more information and is, in most cases, more easily understood than an extensive talk. Children cannot concentrate for long periods of time and the coach should keep his introduction to a minimum so that activity commences as quickly as possible.

It is very easy to forget something of importance when teaching, so to diminish the chance of this a set order of routine should always be used.

1. Divide the squad into groups of four, five or six depending upon the total number, the space available and the stroke to be coached. Number each member of the group.
2. The area into which the demonstration stroke will be played is decided and the audience arranged so that they are in no danger.
3. The coach should then draw a crease and the batsman's stance (foot positions) on the ground, with chalk when possible. Alternatively this may be pre-arranged using permanent markings.
4. The coach is now ready to play the

demonstration stroke without a ball. At this point the term length should be made clear (in minimum time) and the stroke performed.

5. The position of the feet at the end of the stroke should be highlighted and these positions traced on the ground.

6. Going back to point 4, any detailed discussion should be the subject of a separate lesson.

Having completed two or three demonstrations without the ball, the coach now arranges a demonstration with the ball, at the same time setting up a group that will help the others learn the principles of group coaching organisation.

Each player in the group will already have been given a number and the coach, as stated, will use one group to set out the apparatus and markings as an example to everyone.

DUTIES WITHIN THE GROUP

No. 1: Batsman – collects a bat and chalk to mark out the areas and foot positions.

No. 2: Bowler – marks out the target for the ball (in co-operation with the batsman) and the bowling position.

No. 3: Feeder – collects balls and keeps a supply ready for the bowler.

Nos. 4 and 5: Fielders – collect skittles, measure out target area, field within it, return balls to feeder.

No. 6: Wicket-keeper – when required, or extra fielder.

DEMONSTRATION WITH A BALL

Temporarily taking the place of the batsman in the demonstration group, the coach will give a demonstration of the stroke after instructing the bowler in two very *important* points.

1. The bowler should say 'bat up' to the batsman and then wait for him to lift the bat to show his readiness. Only then should the bowler deliver the ball. If the calling of 'bat up' is not stressed, the ball will be delivered too frequently with the batsman not ready and the whole practice will fail.

2. It is essential for the bowler to co-operate with the batsman in setting the bowling position and the target to bowl or throw at. Only by spending time getting this right will the particular stroke be practised properly.

The importance of accurate serving/bowling at the right pace cannot be overemphasised in any specific practice.

As soon as the coach has given a suitable demonstration (taking minimum rather than maximum time) the groups should start working in previously selected areas taking safety as a major consideration. After each batsman has had six or seven attempts at the stroke, the group rotates to give everyone an equal opportunity of making progress in a short time. The coach should take extreme care to impart only a little information at one time for the children to assimilate. A whole session of group coaching should never concentrate on more than two or three points of technique.

Fig 11   Mark out the target.

Fig 12   Bat up – and drop the ball.

GRIP, STANCE AND BACKLIFT

In group coaching it is essential to get the groups working as soon as possible, leaving any discussion and instructions on grip, stance and backlift till well into the session. The coach may then stress that all strokes start with a backlift, hence the instruction from the bowler 'bat up'. As for the grip, if the bats are the right weight and size the majority will learn to hold them correctly fairly quickly, although it is always worth a check on this important basic technique. For a concentrated practice of GSB as it will be known, it is always useful to split the groups into pairs for a more detailed assessment of their abilities.

There are just one or two further points to remember:

* Plan your group coaching session for enjoyment and learning.
* Make sure your groups start work together.
* Never stop a group unless you know *exactly* what you are going to say.
* When you *do* have something to say, make sure you are in the *right position* to say it.
* Think safety.

GROUP COACHING: BATTING LAYOUT

Good serving is essential. Vary serving position if necessary to achieve correct bounce. The target in the back strokes is approximate, the server throwing the ball down the arrow. The target in the drives is exact and marked for each batsman. The server drops the ball from eye level. The batsman drives the ball on the second bounce. Never allow fielders within ten paces of batsmen for attacking strokes. Fielders should change sides if necessary and field the rebound.

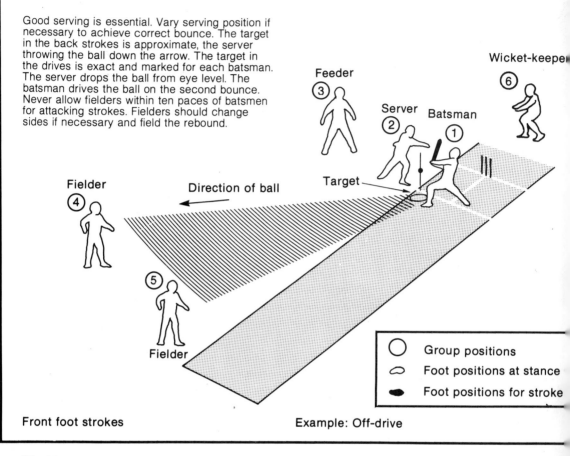

Feeder
③

Wicket-keeper
⑥

Server ② Batsman ①

Fielder
④

Direction of ball

Target

Fielder
⑤

○ Group positions
⌒ Foot positions at stance
● Foot positions for stroke

Front foot strokes

Example: Off-drive

Fig 13

BOWLING

As in batting, the foundations of the group coaching practice will be in the specific sequence of explanation, demonstration and repetition.

1. To assess the task and its planning, the coach should divide the group into pairs and without any tuition whatsoever get them to bowl to each other, noting those who may need special help later.
2. The pairs of players should face each other across the room, or if outdoors about fifteen to twenty paces apart. It is a good teaching point to ensure that left arm bowlers are on the left of the coach as he faces a particular line of players, as this enables them to see him more easily. The coach should then demonstrate 'the coil' (Fig 15) and get all the players to adopt this position. This is the only occasion when players are held for any length of time in a static position during the teaching of bowling. From 'the coil' they should swing the front arm out and down towards their partner, whilst at the same

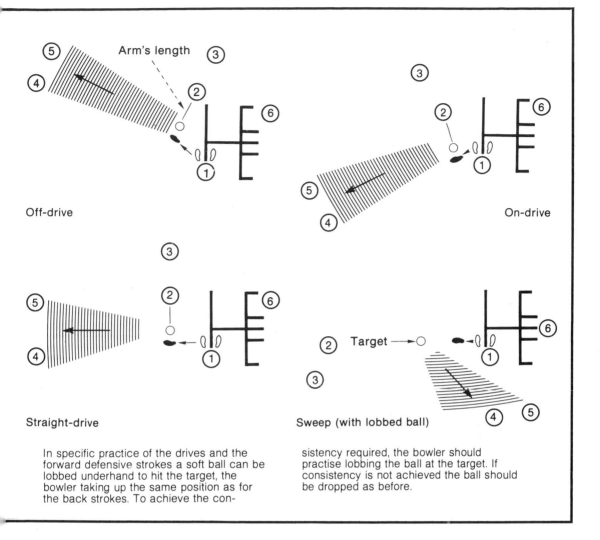

Off-drive

On-drive

Arm's length

Straight-drive

Sweep (with lobbed ball)

In specific practice of the drives and the forward defensive strokes a soft ball can be lobbed underhand to hit the target, the bowler taking up the same position as for the back strokes. To achieve the con-

sistency required, the bowler should practise lobbing the ball at the target. If consistency is not achieved the ball should be dropped as before.

time, the bowling arm swings completely round, with a 'windmill' action, starting from the chin. The coach should emphasise the following points:

*   Look behind the high front arm at your partner with the back slightly arched.
*   Lean back, away from your partner, and then swing towards him. Swing the arms – no jerking.

3. As soon as the coach is satisfied that the coil position and the swinging action

of the arms are correct, he should introduce a ball into the activity. Points to remember at this stage are:

*   The ball should be held in the fingers and not in the palm of the hand.
*   The ball should hit the ground before reaching the receiver.

This is all the information necessary to start the group bowling. Other information relating to the complete action is introduced as soon as the coach feels that the group as a whole can cope with it.

BACK STROKES

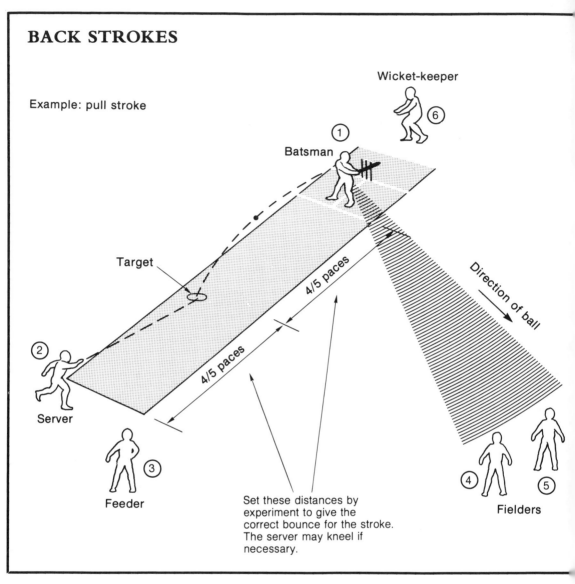

Example: pull stroke

Wicket-keeper ⑥

① Batsman

Target

4/5 paces

4/5 paces

Direction of ball

② Server

4/5 paces

③ Feeder

Set these distances by experiment to give the correct bounce for the stroke. The server may kneel if necessary.

④ ⑤ Fielders

Fig 14

Remember again, that too much inform-ation in a short time only serves to confuse and can have a detrimental effect on the whole coaching programme.

The Run-up

The next step is to introduce the run-up, with a thorough explanation of its function.

To establish a good movement from the run-up into the delivery stride, the coach must very quickly and firmly establish how the young bowler will end the run-up with a jump or 'bound' as we will call it. The coach will demonstrate 'the bound' by running two or three strides before taking off and landing – always aiming to land on the foot adja-cent to his bowling arm, i.e. right arm bowlers take off from the left foot and land on the right, vice versa for left arm

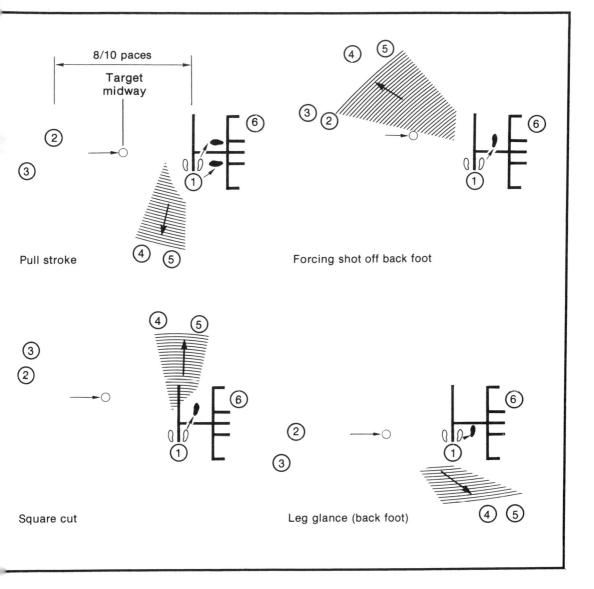

Pull stroke

Forcing shot off back foot

Square cut

Leg glance (back foot)

bowlers.

The group should now perform this activity several times, following each other, in turn, across the room or field. This important movement should be carefully checked at this stage as any bad habits, such as hopping or jumping off the wrong foot will be very difficult to correct later.

The next step is to introduce a ninety degree turn whilst in the air, so that on landing, the foot concerned (right for right arm bowlers) is at right angles to the direction of forward movement. This is a very important position to establish in bowling as it enables the bowler to achieve the classic *sideways on* position to the batsman.

Following the successful imitation of the coach demonstrating this action, the group will move on to landing in the coil position where they should try to pause

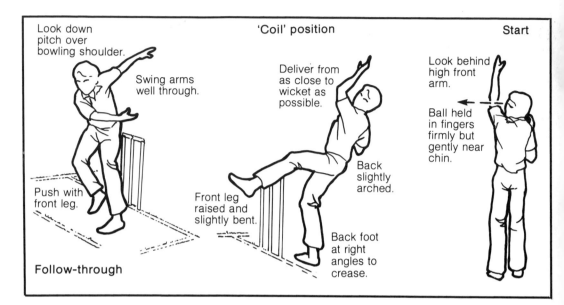

Fig 15 The 'coil' position.

Fig 16   The bound.

before running on. To hold the coil position for a second or two it is necessary to lean well back from the intended direction of the ball, as you land with your foot parallel to the crease.

The teaching of the run-up is now complete and the whole action should be practised by the group: *run – bound – land in the coil position – bowl – follow through.* The *follow-through* is also an integral and important part of the total action and should be vigorous and complete in its performance.

POINTS SYSTEMS

There are various competitive points systems for bowling that can be used to stimulate interest. For beginners, points should be scored for hitting a length target and also the wickets. When the bowlers have gained some degree of success they should be encouraged to try to bowl a particular type of ball and obtain another point if the ball moves in the correct manner. It is very important that players who are trying to become spin bowlers should practise their spinning technique as soon as their bowling action is satisfactory. It is of little use to be able to bowl a line and length but not be able to pitch the ball when trying to spin it.

Target positions need to be varied so that each type of bowler learns to pitch the ball in the correct area for the ball to be most effective, for example, off-spinners must pitch outside or on the off-stump. Faster bowlers will have their target a greater distance from the batsman than slower bowlers. One further consideration is the allowance the coach makes for the age or physique of his bowlers with regard to the pitch length.

The Five Basic Positions

In the early 1950s three great men of cricket were involved in setting up the first ever National Coaching Scheme. They were G.O. (Gubby) Allen, Harry Altham and Harry Crabtree, now legendary figures in the history of coaching cricket. Whilst Harry Crabtree worked on establishing the principles of group coaching, Gubby Allen and Harry Altham concerned themselves with the production of the first MCC coaching book.

Brilliant in its conception, this remarkable book of the time very clearly described the distilled knowledge of some of the finest cricketers in the country. Contained in this knowledge was the idea of giving coaches a series of pictures on which a good bowling action could be based. Whilst other basic actions have produced good results in isolation, the basic action defined in the five basic positions decided upon has stood the test of time and to my mind is worth repeating for any aspiring coach to digest. Imagine that the positions described are frames from a moving picture. If you can, these pictures 'in the mind', so to speak, can be your biggest single asset in the coaching of bowling. When you have assimilated the following descriptions and drawings, if you get the opportunity compare them with Patrick Eagar's classical sequence of Denis Lillee on pages 48 to 53 of *The Skills of Cricket*. This sequence of the great bowler will never be bettered, neither will the basic idea conceived so long ago by Gubby Allen and his team. It is with pride that I reproduce this original sequence, with the kind permission of MCC.

Position 1

Position 2

Position 3

Position 4

Position 5

Position 1 The bound. Just after the jump off the left foot, the position is created by turning the left shoulder towards the batsman, with the left arm reaching upwards. The right foot lands in a vital position parallel to the crease.

Position 2 Landing on the right foot, the arch of the back and the leaning away from the batsman virtually 'cock the spring' to give the delivery its maximum potential. This is the well-known 'coil' position.

Position 3 Everything needs to be sideways in this position, giving maximum body action to the delivery. The length of the stride varies with the type of bowler. Too long a stride loses height, too short a stride loses balance. Care should be taken not to take the left foot across the right foot if you are looking for maximum pace, as this produces a blocking action of the follow-through. Neither should it be splayed out.

Position 4 The body should now be pivoting round the left side, all weight being rapidly transferred to the left foot. It should be possible to reach maximum delivery height in this position. Eyes should still be looking down the pitch as the ball is released.

Position 5 The start of the vital follow-through. There should still be plenty of impetus in the action at this stage. The right shoulder will be pointing down the pitch and the bowler will again be looking directly over it. Both arms will have swung right through to complete the delivery.

Note For the coach to be able to analyse the action properly, several deliveries should be studied, isolating the position concerned in each delivery.

Fig 17   The five basic positions.

FIELDING

Compared to batting and bowling, fielding in general is a simpler activity for group coaching. In fact one might relate the team in the field, as a unit or part of a unit, to a group coaching situation.

Any particular fielding skill can be practised effectively without considering the use of nets. Groups of two or more can involve themselves in a variety of ways stopping, intercepting, retrieving or catching the ball. Specialist fielders such as the slips, or cover fielders with a little imagination can set up worthwhile practices, which can be analysed in the same way as batting or bowling. There are many fielding skill practices that can be designed as a useful and enjoyable competitive game, either in a single fielding session or as a warm-up activity in a general coaching programme or session. A few examples are described in Chapter 9. I am personally very keen on using a competitive game in the group coaching of fielding as it is again an area that can very effectively put players under the necessary harmless pressure for them to show worthwhile improvement quickly, whilst at the same time giving the coach a good indication of fitness levels. Many is the time I have seen a player retrieve and throw a ball in brilliantly when there is nothing at stake, but when 'the chips have been down' the same player has both muffed the pick-up and the throw. In my experience, well set-up group fielding practices can help improve attitude and confidence to an astonishing degree.

Fig 18 Team fielding practice, immediately before the match.
This is essential for a team to acclimatise to the ground
environment. (U11 Festival, Edgbaston)

WICKET-KEEPING

This is perhaps the least coached and
practised part of cricket. Most wicket-
keepers I know have spent more time
batting or bowling in practice sessions
than wicket-keeping. In fact, I know of
hardly any wicket-keeper who genuinely
practises at all. Mind you, the odds are
well stacked against him. Usually the nets
are put up and the practice wicket laid out
without leaving any real space for the

wicket-keeper to practise the art – and
then we wonder why early in the next
match the wicket-keeper misses an 'easy'
chance!

Being realistic and with a little planning, it is a very simple group coaching
exercise to bowl to your wicket-keeper in
a way that will give him most help. Either
without a batsman in the net or preferably with a batsman playing and missing
to pre-arranged instruction from the
coach. Crash mats are a good method of

Fig 19   Group coaching: wicket-keeping practice. Batsman
        'playing and missing' deliberately.

giving wicket-keepers diving practice, by throwing the wide catches over the mat, and not just once or twice! I hope I have made the point. I am surprised bowlers do not insist on it, and it would be quite easy to combine bowling and wicket-keeping practice as part of the coaching session – batsmen are not the only players in the team. As in fielding practices, the NCA's Proficiency Awards Scheme provides excellent group practice for wicket-keepers.

Fig 20   David Gower (England)

3 Net Coaching

Traditionally, net coaching has been the main if not the only source of sophisticated cricket coaching and until the development of group coaching it was the only means of giving uninterrupted cricket coaching in reasonable conditions. As a direct result of net coaching and practice, conscientious batsmen have been able to progress comparatively quickly in acquiring skills. This view is supported by the very high percentage of Test and county batsmen that have been produced, particularly between the wars, by public schools and, to a limited degree, grammar schools of the time. Good net facilities and coaching expertise were part of the sporting heritage of these schools and whilst grammar schools, as such, are no longer with us, the public schools carry on the traditions and still produce excellent cricketers. Whilst the same cannot be said of the state schools, the success of the English Schools Cricket Association (who draw the majority of their players at county and national level from the state schools) disproves the oft-quoted comment that *no* cricket is being played in the state schools. In fact, many ESCA players attending state schools are linked to the thriving cricket club scene, throughout the country, where nets, good wickets and good coaching are becoming increasingly more available. It is obvious that club cricket helps school cricket and vice versa.

In theory it is very difficult to argue against net coaching being the most effective form of coaching individual players, but in practice there are many factors that need to be considered before this comment can be substantiated. Firstly the net wicket (pitch) needs to be well prepared, helping the bowler to a minimal degree; in other words, a 'good batting wicket'. Secondly, a 'net' needs to be well organised by the coach to get the most out of the session for all those participating. Unless everyone in the net is approaching the session in the right way with the coach not only 'in charge' but also seen to be, the practice will deteriorate and consequently be of little value. At its best, net coaching and practice is probably the most effective long-term method of improving batsmen and bowlers. At its worst it is the most overrated pastime, doing far more harm than good.

When coaching children, *before* they commence work in the nets it is a considerable advantage for them to have followed a *basic group coaching programme* in the skills of cricket.

Pre-net Requirements

Whether indoors or outdoors check that:

1. Batting surface is in good condition (roll if necessary).
2. Bowlers' run-ups are satisfactory and safe.
3. Netting is safe – no holes, no excessive billowing in double nets (use canvas reinforcement if necessary).
4. Pitch length is correct and all creases

Fig 21   Net practice can be pleasant – make sure it is effective. (Lords)

marked, and that guy ropes, when used, are properly located.
5. Satisfactory lighting is available, including background vision.
6. Suitable equipment is available – bats, balls, wickets and so on.
7. When using video recording equipment, a position is established in good time.

With Players Available

Decide upon the allocation of time for each player, both in batting and bowling, then set the order of batting and bowling. Be certain all players are fully informed of safety procedures and regulations. In particular, ensure that players face the batting area at all times, even when walking back to the bowling mark. When batting, collect stray balls from the side netting using the bat and not the hand – keep the head well clear of the side netting. No more than three bowlers (absolute maximum, four) should operate in one net.

The coach must remember to:

1. Ensure that players of a similar age and ability are, as far as possible, grouped together.
2. Give wicket-keepers proper practice and ensure that there is enough space behind the wicket to accommodate wicket-keepers.
3. Prevent bowlers from going up the net to collect balls until the sequence of bowlers has been completed and all balls are 'dead'.
4. Instruct young players to lob the balls back to the bowlers only when a sequence has been completed. Older players can, perhaps, speed the service up, under the direction of the coach.
5. Encourage players, particularly bowlers, to warm up before practice, just as they would before a game.
6. Minimise talk and maximise action.

Fig 22 Coach and player. In this situation the coach must
know his subject completely if he is to be worthy of the
name.

Just Prior to Practice

Coaches restate the importance of safety,
reminding the batsmen of the need to
wear protective equipment and remove
jewellery (watches, rings and so on).
Stress the very real danger from adjacent
nets. Whilst bowlers mark out their run-
ups, batsmen take 'guard'. The coach will
have decided previously the type of net
session, i.e. teaching or coaching net.

NET ROUTINES

As in every aspect of the coach's work,
pre-planning will play an important part
in all net practices. Consideration will

need to have been given to the number
and type of players involved, the time
available, the net conditions and so on. If
a player is experienced and his progress is
being monitored there must be continuity from the previous coaching session.
(Watch existing video or other records of
the player.) The coach may, for example,
be working on one single batting point.
If this is so, the net session will need to
be specific in its purpose. It will certainly
be of no use if the weakness concerned is
to do with off-driving say, and the bowlers continually bowl short. In other
words, for a percentage of a batsman's
net-time, under instructions from the
coach, the bowlers will endeavour to
bowl at his weakness.

If a batsman is new to a coach the first consideration will be a general survey, backed by a video recording if possible. Only then will one or two points be considered in any one session. Net sessions that come under these headings may be termed *coaching nets*. Coaching or coaches can easily get a bad name if just one coach 'rushes in' and takes it upon himself to identify and correct, in ten minutes, the dozens of faults he thinks a player may have!

When a net session concerns a young player and an entirely new skill is to be taught, the coach will be working on only one coaching point at a time after previously having gone through the 'teaching a skill' process. This net session would be termed a *teaching net*.

There are, of course, many combinations a coach may design to cover any requirement of a player within the net.

A Possible Teaching Net Routine: Batsman

1. The batsman plays himself in, the coach advises the bowlers.
2. The coach watches the batsman. Knowing the stroke he is teaching, the coach will quickly decide on the particular coaching point to be worked upon.
3. Having decided upon the coaching point, the coach takes the bowlers down the net to listen and observe. He instructs the batsman in general on the stroke concerned and gives a demonstration. He serves for the batsman to play the stroke, highlighting the coaching point decided upon.
4. For a short time the bowlers attempt to bowl to this stroke, the coach commenting as necessary.
5. Then follows free practice.

6. After that, a target game is played (a run target from a set number of deliveries).

A Possible Coaching Net Routine: Batsman

1. If the coach does not know the batsman some prior homework should have been done. If neither, the net should be simply a 'recording' session, in preparation for the next net with the same player.
2. Assuming a knowledge of the batsman, the coach will (acting as a captain) discuss with the bowlers a possible weakness of the batsman as he plays himself in. They will then look to bowl to that weakness.
3. Knowing the weakness the bowlers are bowling to, the coach will now work exclusively with the batsman on improving technique for the one stroke only.
4. After a good coaching period, free batting practice will be allowed, giving the coach time to work with the bowlers.
5. There is little point in a target game in this coaching situation with the experienced batsman.

A teaching or coaching net can, of course, be easily set up for individual bowlers.

REMEMBER

All the coach's remarks should be as encouraging as possible. For beginners, almost every ball bowled merits a comment from the coach, either on the success of the ball or on the missing of the stroke, or on both. Generally, all comments should be audible to both batsmen and bowlers. Since praise tends to reinforce a skill, adverse criticism can destroy a skill and comments at this stage should en-

Fig 23   Phil Edmonds of England and Middlesex shows by the quality of his action that net practice is important to him.

courage. Experienced players need far less in the way of comment, and praise should be limited to a good performance.

As each batsman completes his net time, the coach should take him aside and give a summary of his performance, indicating the main point to be worked on during practice time in the immediate future. Similar comments should be made to bowlers.

Division of Net Time

Ensure that everyone attending the net session is allocated a period of coaching and free practice time commensurate with their role as a player. That is, be realistic. Whilst it is desirable to give your No. 11 batsman batting practice and a certain amount of coaching, recognise that coaching time (the coach's time) is valuable enough to make the most of it where and with whom it will count the most – also bear in mind the requirements of the *team*. Coaches cannot afford favourites.

Think in terms of a batsman's time in the net being divisible into three parts:

1. Ten to twenty per cent – playing in.
2. Fifty to sixty per cent – coaching.
3. Thirty to forty per cent – free practice.

Thus in a twenty minute 'net' the batsman could have four minutes of playing in, ten minutes of coaching and six minutes of free practice.

CONCLUSION

These notes on net practice and coaching very clearly highlight the importance of good organisation. I am sure that most coaches will agree that much can be done in this field of coaching. Planning the whole and concentration on detail are the keys to success. I have earlier mentioned how good nets and expert coaching at school have contributed to the development of very good cricketers in the past. What I did not say was: how many cricketers have been lost through *not* having these advantages?

Net practice and coaching should be *fun* for everyone, but the player should recognise the practice for what it is: a serious attempt to improve technique and consequently performance – when it counts – *in a match*.

Fig 24   Vivian Richards (West Indies)

4 Middle Practice and Coaching

For some reason or other, practising and coaching in the match situation, on a normal match wicket with lots of space around it, seems to be something of a Cinderella exercise. As mentioned previously, the popular idea of practice and coaching seems to centre on the practice nets – maybe through tradition, maybe as a result of the mistaken idea that the match square should be reserved for the official matches only. What a pity if this is the case. With a little more thought and planning the most effective practice of all, both individually and as a team, can take place in conditions not that much different from the real thing. Of course, if the number of match wickets available on the square are restricted it may not be possible, or fair, to expect the groundsman to release his 'pride and joy' for anything but the match itself.

Even so, this should not prohibit the possibility of middle practice and coaching. The day following the big match is ideal for giving the juniors a test on the match wicket used. Seldom will it have deteriorated to any serious degree. Better still, a non-turf (artificial) wicket could be laid on the edge of the square. If I was asked what is the best investment a club could make in its future, without hesitation I would put the non-turf match wicket very high on the list. Why? Here are a few reasons for this:

* The future of any cricket club is linked with its membership at all ages. Without question a really thriving club is a club with an active junior section supported by good supervision and facilities. Clubs subscribing to this view create a snowball effect on membership as parents of juniors become involved in the life of the club and a family spirit prevails.

* It is noticeable also that those clubs providing excellent all-round facilities for members are usually successful on the field. They attract the better players in the area.

* This line of comment may sound remote from the subject of middle practice but it is not really, as teams that enjoy playing together also enjoy practising together. The wheel turns full circle and success breeds success!

* Team fielding practice becomes far more realistic when conducted in match play circumstances and that most neglected of subjects, the coaching of captaincy, takes on a whole new perspective. Different tactics can be tried out, field placings experimented with and the experience of decision making does our young captains no harm at all. Batting skills can be tested against true field placings and that frustrating aspect of junior and youth cricket, running between wickets, can be experienced and improved upon without regret. Wicket-keepers for once become an integral

Fig 25   With the coach as umpire, here is an ideal example of
middle practice.

part of a practice session, as they try out new facets of their individual roles without the pressures of the 'once only' chances of a match. Even umpires and scorers, those dedicated and vital people of cricket, will appreciate the opportunity of sharpening their concentration in a practice match.

At the beginning of the season, middle practice and the practice match are, in my opinion, a must, just prior to the commencement of the official programme of matches. It is never a bad idea to split the potential first and second elevens on these occasions. Let the potential first team attack bowl at the likely first team batsmen and the potential second team bowlers bowl to the possible second team batsmen. Coaches should make time to repeat this process during the season, it is the one way of comparing 'like with like' and an excellent pointer to final team selection. Incidentally the first team captain should take charge of the first team bowling attack in these matches.

Here are some further ideas as to how one might further benefit from team middle practice:

*   Let the good coach set a defensive field and the batting side practise the 'run chase' in different combinations of runs required against overs available.
*   Let the batting side practise hitting sixes (and fours) against a defensive field. You may find another Ian Botham – who knows? Some of the players will quickly realise the futility of hitting the ball in the air. Alternatively they will realise that to hit the ball consistently for four or six is not a matter of brute force but more of a sound technique allied to controlled strength. It may even persuade batsmen to go in for special strength training; other sportsmen do.
*   If the success rate is very low in the previous practice, turn the whole into a group coaching exercise, serving/throwing or bowling the ball to give the batsman a real opportunity of 'whacking' it. Experiencing the feeling of only one successful hit will give a batsman confidence when it counts! Take a tip from other sports. Can you imagine Seve Ballesteros not practising his driving, or the heavyweight champion of the world not using a punch bag?
*   Having said this, the situation may be entirely different. One could be involved in a Roses Match and be the last man at the wicket, with no chance of winning and two overs to go. A good defensive technique and experience in this type of finish (match or practice match) is worth having. The good coach can make a tight finish in a practice match almost the equivalent of the real thing.
*   Bowling and fielding to win in varying circumstances can also be very tense and just as important as batting to win. It is not surprising that a bowler suddenly loses his direction or length, or both, when experiencing a challenge he has never met before, whether it be at the end, the beginning or throughout the match. How can a spin bowler expect to bowl a team out on a spinner's wicket if he has never bowled on one before – or at least for quite a long time?

Whenever you can, be sure in the course of all your middle practice, whether it be batting, bowling or fielding, to simulate the conditions that may be required for success.

Finally, remember that if you are the coach in charge of the middle practice it is not a bad idea to officiate from the position normally occupied by the umpire at the bowler's end. If you are lucky enough to have umpires, vary your own position in the field to suit the job in hand, whether it be studying your wicket-keeper's technique or discussing tactics with your captain.

Fig 26   Allan Border (Australia)

5 Skill Analysis

I can think of a few cricket coaches who will think I have taken leave of my senses, coming up with such a title when referring to cricket! Nevertheless, for some time I have felt that a more scientific view of fault finding in coaching could pay dividends. Now, after a reasonable amount of experiment with my colleagues in NCA, I am convinced it is a way ahead. Having said this, bear in mind that skill analysis, albeit under a different name, has been used by coaches, to some extent, since coaching began. After all, it is only watching a player performing a particular skill, identifying what and why that player may be doing well or not so well and, if the latter, coming up with a cure. In fact, we are observing, recording, analysing and assessing a player's performance and then if possible, in co-operation with the player, correcting technique or attitude if necessary, to produce an improved performance. This is the skill of any coach worthy of the name.

However, our technological age has now given coaches, not only more advanced methods of observing their players, but more sophisticated methods of recording what they see or even what they don't see! With the human memory being highly fallible, this ability to record not only what the eye can see but also what it cannot see is probably the major step forward in coaching in recent years. I am, of course, referring to the movie or video film camera combined with the slow motion video playback facility, which is now so readily available.

In the past, how on earth did coaches correctly diagnose a fault that could not properly be seen, let alone recorded? Yet somehow they did, maybe through pure instinct. When one thinks of the successful coaching that has taken place for so long it is indeed amazing and a great credit to the dedicated few, who have loyally pursued their vocations with little recognition and without anything like the support we have today.

Looking at other sports whose end results are more measurable than cricket and whose coaches in general seem to be more technically advanced, there is no doubt that it is time we put our house in order – or at least had a look at what might be done. We really do need to use the facilities and equipment that we have to do a better job – and a better job means better players at all levels of the game, whether it be in Test cricket, schools cricket or club cricket.

APPLYING SKILL ANALYSIS

Firstly study in depth *all* the skills of cricket in so far as you can. Watch the game closely on film, television or preferably live. Watching players at close quarters in net practice can be invaluable in learning about the skills. Carefully read the leading coaching publications. It is likely, but not certain, that if you are fortunate enough to have been a gifted player, you will have a depth of knowledge of the skills you were best at. This may lead to specialisation, but look again and again at all aspects of coaching the game before you begin to specialise. Knowledge in isolation can sometimes do more harm than good. Retrace your steps, discuss the game and coaching with those you respect most. After all, a lot of water may have passed under the bridge since you were last really involved. You will need an *open* mind and one that can change if you are to be a good coach. On occasions you will need to admit you are wrong. Remember also that skill analysis is not about performing yourself – although a good demonstration will always be worth a thousand words.

Looking in the future, let us assume you are now, if you were not before, well versed in *all* the skills of cricket, even with a special knowledge of some of them. You may even think you are able to recognise *all* the possible flaws in those skills. *Don't you believe it*! Some, yes, but the small, subtle flaws that can develop in a player will need to be pointed out again and again. More often than not they really do need some spotting. Do not be fooled by the obvious – it may be a result, not a cause.

Observation

Observation is very much the name of the game. You need lots of practice in doing nothing but look for the obvious flaws and, progressively, the less obvious; in other words, getting right down to the detail contained in every skill, so that you will know almost instinctively when they are being performed incorrectly. Some of the working coaches I know are really amazing in this field – but it is something you need to continually work at.

FAULT FINDING

Having now observed the skills in action and identified even the most subtle of faults, you may think that you have arrived – again, *don't you believe it*! Having spotted the fault, the next and most difficult step is establishing why it is occurring. You may know, but not necessarily, as one fault can so easily be caused by another.

Let us look at an example. A batsman is continually hitting the ball in the air on the leg-side and as a result is regularly being caught out early in his innings. You may recognise that he is trying to play that most difficult of strokes, the on-drive. Almost immediately you realise that he cannot play the stroke properly as in his stance and in the playing of the stroke his head is leaning far too much towards off-side, throwing him off balance as soon as he moves to drive. This is very often the reason for the fault – but there may be others. For example, could it be a faulty grip? That is, are the 'vees' not in line on the bat handle as the stroke is commenced? As a result of a weak top hand grip, does the bottom hand overpower the top hand, closing the face of the bat and pulling it across the line of the ball? Maybe the front hip is not opening slightly on the downswing or possibly the front shoulder not leading into the stroke is the root of the problem?

Let me give you another example, this time with bowling. Norman Cowans (England and Middlesex) is a very successful pace bowler, particularly at county level. However, at times under pressure, he loses pace for some reason and unaccountably bowls down the leg-side when bowling to a right-handed batsman. Who knows what the trouble

Fig 27 Norman Cowans – this position shows how Norman sometimes loses pace and accuracy. He has lost his 'spring' (lean away from the batsman) long before delivering the ball.

is? Is he concentrating? Is he fit? A host of questions, some of them unfair to say the least, are asked by all sorts of so-called experts, as is very often the case.

In my opinion, Norman's problem is that he simply does not establish the necessary lean-away from the batsman (common to most of the very best fast bowlers) as he lands in the delivery stride. If he doesn't get this position right (sometimes he does) he will lose pace. Of this there can be no doubt – 'the trigger is not fully cocked'. Norman then searches for pace without the body action that the

'lean-away' would give him. This opens his chest to the batsman in the effort to get his arm through quicker, causing him to bowl with the arm and without the body, pushing the ball into the batsman, and very often down the leg-side as a consequence.

The naked eye could not catch the detail necessary for the general observer to appreciate these comments. I was, in fact, very fortunate to have made a number of coaching films with Norman Cowans and the slow motion sequences in these films very clearly establish the points I have made. Norman has a lean-away almost in the class of Denis Lillee and Michael Holding at their best, but unfortunately he doesn't hold it long enough and by the time he lands in the delivery stride he is practically vertical.

I suspect this half-way position (call it what you like) in Norman's case is a result of trying to bowl too fast. He looks as though he is trying to obtain the run-up speed of Malcolm Marshall, the fine West Indian fast bowler, who is a much smaller man with a completely different physical make-up and a strong arm, rather than a strong body, action. My remedy would be to slow Norman down just a fraction as he comes into the delivery stride. A gathering, almost a 'moving pause', if there can be such a thing, giving him a fraction longer to fully 'cock the trigger' and 'sight the target!' Am I right or wrong; who knows? One thing is certain, without the film equipment and the will to record Norman's action I could never have put the case forward for you to consider.

From these examples it is obvious that specific combinations of observation, recording, analysis and assessment are a prime requisite of skill analysis. Even a

Fault Identification Chart (Batting)

Name of player:
Name of coach: Date:
Skill:

	Head Eyes	Shoul-ders	Arms	Hands	Bat	Hips	Knees	Feet	Comment (against x)
Grip									
Stance								X	Feet too wide apart
Backlift									
Downswing		X							No leading with front shoulder
Point of contact									
Weight transfer									
Follow-through									

Initial fault (problem):

Possible reasons:

Information transferred to:

Fig 28

very fast film used with a motor-driven still camera (35mm) can produce interesting results. A number of sequences are shown in Figs 31 to 34, together with appropriate comments. These again, whilst not so good as the video system, do take some of the guesswork out of analysis. From these sequences the message is clear – many questions need to be answered if any real progress is to be made. Some sort of recording system in which relevant information on the player and the skill in question can be noted is essential.

On occasions, of course, the experienced coach can go straight to the heart of the problem and simply tell the player what is wrong and how to put it right. This method may be acceptable for a casual coaching session, but in a sophisticated coaching environment it is an approach that I do not favour. It leaves too much to chance, and experience tells me that it seldom works.

I favour a recording system that can be completed in a logical sequence and used effectively when summarising a player's ability and potential. A number of sys-

Fault Identification Chart (Bowling)

Name of player:
Name of coach: **Date:**
Skill:

	Head	Shoulders	Non-bowling arm	Bowling arm	Wrist	Back	Knees	Feet	Comment (against x)
Grips									
Run-up								X	Strides too short
Position 1 (bound)									
Position 2 (coil)									
Position 3 (delivery stride)			X						Little use of front arm
Position 4 (delivery)									
Position 5 (begin follow-through)									
Follow-through (completed)									

Initial fault (problem):

Possible reasons:

Information transferred to:

Fig 29

tems have been devised, but invariably coaches prefer to develop their own. The important thing is for the reports and records to be very clear, with sufficient detail to enable them to be properly interpreted by other coaches without discussion. Obviously the future in this field must be with computers (we are not far from it now); then coaching can really come into its own.

Figs 28 and 29 give examples of how a player's technique can be observed and analysed. These forms can be particularly useful when transferring and collating

---

Player   **Occasion/Course Details**

Name: Description:
Address: Venue:

                                         Dates:
Tel. No: Coach:
Date of Birth: Address:
Club/School:
Recommended by: Tel. No:

Conditions of Assessment (i.e. type of wicket, etc.)

Coach's Summary and Recommendations

Skill Assessment – Bowling

Grips (basic/spin/swing)
Run-up (including bound)
Delivery (consider positions 2/3/4)
Follow-through
Control/variation of pace/degree of swing/spin, etc.
Attitude and application (including comment of fielding ability)

Skill Assessment – Batting

Grip
Stance
Backlift
Back defence
Forward defence
Attacking back strokes (including cuts/forcing shot/pull/hook/leg glance)
Attacking forward strokes (including drives/sweep/leg glance)
Attitude and application (including comment of fielding ability)

Signature .... Date ....

Fig 30

visual information (video recordings) for extended use to other assessment records (Fig 30). Remember to look beyond the obvious. Be prepared to relate your thinking to that of the player. It is likely that by listening to the player's comments on his own performance, clues will be given to possible faults. This is an area often neglected by the inexperienced coach.

EXAMPLES OF SKILL ANALYSIS RECORDING

Fig 31 Back foot not landing parallel enough to the crease, making it difficult to see over the shoulder.

Fig 32 Not a bad delivery position, but probably just too much flex in the front leg for the speed of delivery.

Fig 33 Good head position in follow-through, but bowling arm not taken far enough through.

Bowling (Figs 31 to 33)

Grip (basic/swing/spin) Left arm over, in-swing. Good, but ball could be held more towards the end of the fingers rather than the palm.

Run-up Generally smooth and economical, only occasionally hurrying too much.

Delivery Poor use of front arm, but quick arm action. Head quite often falls away. Sometimes a good sideways position but not consistently.

Follow-through Quite often limited due to head falling away.

Control/variation of pace/degree of spin, swing, etc. No apparent swing, checked finger position. Using poor ball and with better ball could get it to swing occasionally.

Attitude and application Blowing heavily and fitness needs to be worked upon. Despite this worked very hard, listened, and showed an improvement.

Coach's summary and recommendations Has learned to swing the ball more by easing it more towards the fingertips. Must continue to get the front arm up and fire down the target line, keeping head level throughout. Also general fitness needs improving. He must concentrate on landing with his back foot parallel to the crease when in practice. This young man has something upon which to work.

45

Fig 34 An excellent stance, with head over the line of the stumps, eyes level and relaxed at the knees.

CORRECTION OF FAULTS

We now come to the next step in our endeavours. How does a player change a technique acquired over many years? How does a player under pressure or on the spur of the moment react differently to what instinct and training dictate? Not easily and certainly not overnight! I have heard some amazing comments at the highest levels of the game on what amusingly in this instance may be termed 'correction of faults'. Once, for example, I heard a Test selector (maybe with tongue in cheek) suggest that he would sort out an 'out of form' batsman's technical problem in a five-minute net about an hour before the start of a Test match.

Batting (Fig 34)

Grip Excellent.
Stance Stands tall, head over the line of the stumps, eyes level, relaxed at the knees. Excellent set-up.
Backlift High, early and straight.
Back defence Initially spoilt by early commitment to front foot, but there was a remarkable improvement after information had been fed to him. He now gets very 'sideways' and uses the crease well.
Forward defence Plays very straight, particularly around the off-stump. Needs just a slightly better head lead to the delivery pitching around middle and leg.
Attacking back strokes Early efforts were poor, but, as in backward defence, there was a remarkable improvement once advice had been given. This resulted in a number of good forcing shots being produced, as was the case when pulling short deliveries.
Attacking forward strokes A very good driver of the ball. A number of clean hits were produced, especially through mid-off. When attempting on-drives he fell a little to the off. Again, this was improved with a better head lead.
Attitude and application Looks a player who responds very quickly to advice. Has a good cricket brain and works out quickly what is required of him.
Conditions of assessment Slow to medium pace pitch with variable bounce.
Coach's summary and recommendations Continue to work at back foot play and on-drives. Must allow the ball to come up to him as there is still a tendency to commit himself a little too early on the front foot. His future progress must be carefully watched as he could become an extremely good performer.

The following day he offered the same comment to the opening bowler! Needless to say, however well intended, the offer was valueless. Having made this criticism, I do not wish to confuse the giving of a simple tip with the correction of a basic fault, no matter how small, but in my experience even tips need to be analysed and considered by those involved before putting them into practice. Most of the 'helpful' tips I have heard about, no matter how well meant, seem to be transient, helping the mind rather than the body (although they may be useful to some extent in that sense). Perhaps I am being a bit too sceptical, so let me try and say something constructive. When a fault is virtually ingrained into a player's technique, different courses of action can be taken:

1. Once the player knows what the fault is, its exposure can be minimised providing it is not too basic.
2. The player can live with a basic or trivial fault, and must do, without the concern and maybe trauma of trying to eradicate it. Enjoy what you have, if you can!
3. Make a serious effort to eradicate the fault completely, with the intention of improving performance.

Once the majority of players have reached fifteen or sixteen years of age the 'die is cast' and some combinations of 1 and 2 are generally accepted and a gesture made at 3. If the third course of action is to be attempted properly (and after all this is the real object of the chapter, if not of coaching in general), then the following may produce worthwhile results.

WILL POWER

A supreme effort of will power (with the coach supervising or taking video film). Let the player try to *slowly* perform the correct movement within the skill as a whole for countless repetitions (thousands not hundreds), gradually building the movement up to a normal speed. This is a long, arduous job, even for the smallest change in technique, with no guarantee of success. Early in the process, shape the movement accurately without a

ball, with the coach using the 'pipe cleaner' method (Fig 35), then progress to alternating with a ball and finally use the ball only. If the video film shows that little progress has been made using a ball only, start again from the beginning, again slowly shaping the skill under supervision.

As a coach, be certain to give your player the experience of being in the right position at various points of the skill by physically shaping him into these positions. I call this the 'pipe cleaner' method. (Pipe cleaners are fabric-covered wires that can be 'shaped' as required to suit the bends and angles of the pipe to be cleaned.) If a player hasn't experienced the feeling of being in the correct position, it is

Fig 35   Les Lenham – a great exponent of 'pipe cleaner' instruction – gives a young batsman the feeling of where his head should be when driving.

unlikely that he will know when he has achieved it. However, the coach should appreciate the physical limitations of individuals. For example, as much as I should like to, there is no way I (and a few more chaps I can think of) can finish a drive like Ian Botham or Seve Ballesteros, and if any coach of cricket or golf tried to put me in such positions, they would be attempting the impossible – unquestionably I should break!

ISOLATION

Another method that may be progressively linked to the previous routine is in isolating the part of the skill that needs to be changed, so that any new or improved movement is practised, and hopefully set, in isolation. For example, if a bowler wishes to practise the bowling arm action only, he can sit down and do it, holding the side of the chair with his free arm. Then the complete skill can again be fully practised with the improved movement virtually 'grafted' in the total skill. Whilst not requiring quite the same amount of will power as the other, much hard work and concentration is still needed and again there are no guarantees.

I learned this 'isolation of movement' principle from the well-known Olympic athletics coach, Wilf Paish, the man responsible for training gold medallist Tessa Sanderson. The run-up for throwing the javelin is not dissimilar to that for the fast bowler; in some bowlers, notably Jeff Thomson the famous Australian, it is almost identical. Wilf, a very keen cricket fan, has, in fact, designed a number of exercises for bowlers giving this isolated movement practice (Fig 36). I just hope that if the idea catches on with cricketers, they will give it the same amount of effort

Fig 36 Isolating parts of the bowling action will test each part of the action.

and interest that I have seen given by some of our young athletes.

Summarising this section, it seems that whilst there is still a long way to go in the correction of fault procedures, some positive headway is being made. It only remains for the coach to ensure that this headway is a beginning rather than an end and that the correct fault correction procedures developed for a player are again recorded on film and in writing for the benefit of all. This attitude will give continuity and I am told that two heads are better than one – sometimes!

BENEFITS OF SKILL ANALYSIS

Having come well down the road, before proceeding further let me now review some of the benefits that may come from skill analysis.

* A much closer rapport between coach and player becomes possible.
* Time, money and maybe some frustration is saved through detailed skill analysis reports on individual players being available to sources that may use them; selection committees, for example.
* The whole process inspires confidence in a player with its realism.
* Skill analysis exposes poor coaches and coaching methods and takes some of the mythology out of coaching.
* The ability to put skill analysis into operation and demonstrate its effectiveness lifts the status of the cricket coach – or at least it should.
* Skill analysis requires cricket coaches to acquire skills not previously thought necessary. This again raises their status and potential.
* Skill analysis makes coaching cricket more interesting for coach – and player.
* Skill analysis can be used in all aspects of coaching: Proficiency Award Schemes; group and net coaching programmes; junior competitions; county coaching at all levels including first class; Test match briefings and practice days.

Skill analysis reports (Figs 28 to 34) are the culmination of extensive coaching programmes, designed for players of some ability at any age and level of competition. Their prime object is to enable coaches to set realistic improvement targets and help players to achieve them. Linked with comprehensive planning (*see* Chapter 6), this type of coaching tool can play a major part in the development of future excellence in cricket.

SKILL ASSESSMENT COURSE

Whilst skill analysis is at its best when conducted over a period in a one to one player/coach relationship, a modified form of skill analysis can be applied by what could be called a skill assessment course, involving a number of players and coaches. The following is a suggested format for such a course.

A minimum of one hour of personal assessment should be received by each member of a course. Only very good, experienced coaches should be engaged on a course of this type. One coach should never be responsible for more than six players.

The players should be carefully selected to give a balance to the course. One should consider the number of quality nets, the availability of special equipment, such as a bowling machine, video systems and so on. Whilst a course for eight batsmen only *could* be undertaken, it is a far better arrangement if say, four batsmen and up to eight bowlers were the subjects.

Information will be gathered by personal coaches at the beginning of the course. Notebooks, record forms, tape recorders, video equipment, still cameras and so on will be the means of recording.

Very little actual coaching will take place, the object will be to compile a report on each subject's ability (strengths and weaknesses). The report will include comprehensive notes on how a player may improve performance over a specific period.

Possible Format

Times for the following sessions will need to be decided when the course is designed.

1. *Introduction*   Verbal with course folder.
2. *Net practice*   General loosener; no coaching.
3. *General net practice*   Coaches begin to gather information on individual skills of each player; no coaching.
4. *Demonstrations*   No coaching. Video tapes made of each player demonstrating individual skills, i.e. batting and bowling.
5. *Video playback and lecture*   When everyone has been satisfactorily filmed, the whole group will move on to a video playback and lecture by a coach on the subject concerned. All players will get something from this session as a general discussion of technique develops. Be certain to have a chairman in this session.
6. *General net practice*   This time to include fault correction; *one* or *two* coaching points may be worked upon. These general net practice sessions organised at the end of the course will serve as an example for future work.
7. *Refilming and interviews*   Individual skills will be refilmed as required, whilst coaches will conduct interviews on each

player's cricket philosophy as convenient.
8. *Private discussion*   Personal coaches will have private discussion with their players.
9. *Skill assessment forms*   Coaches will complete skill assessment forms after discussion period.

It is emphasised that immediate recording of information should be the main theme of work for the coaches.

The foregoing notes will undoubtedly give coaches with a genuine interest in progress something to think about. I hope so and I hope some of the ideas put forward will stimulate discussion and serious comment.

Recapitulation

Let me just recapitulate on our sequence of skill analysis for coaches.

1. Plan your method of observation, recording, analysis and assessment (ORAA).
2. Observe.
3. Record.
4. Analyse your records in writing.
5. Assess.
6. Compile report.
7. Lay down corrective actions, if required, in writing.
8. Engage in specific practice of corrective actions over a definite period.
9. Compile second (and most important) report by repeating items 2 to 5.

EXPERIMENTAL ANALYSIS CHART (Fig 37)

Looking at the analysis of performance in general, I feel we can go further and become more effective as coaches. The following analysis chart poses a few questions. This is a chart that may give useful information to coaches. It simply identifies each delivery by a bowler and, to some degree, what happens to it when the batsman takes over.

	Good direction	No.	Score	Wide off	No.	Score	Wide leg	No.	Score
Full toss	4·22·4	7	12						
Half volley	212···XW4 ·4·2···	16	15	422MM ·2	7	10			
Good length	···M····· W	10	—	4XX·4X 2X	8	10	XXXXX ··2X	9	2
Short	·······1· 2··2··	15	5	XXXMX4 ·4··	10	8	XX·X· 3X1X	9	4
Long hop	42MM·433	9	16	4··1423 MM·	10	14	····44 ··	8	8
Bouncer	6M·XXX· XW	9	16	XXXX	4	—	XX4M.M	7	4
Total		66	54		39	42		33	18

Fig 37 Experimental analysis chart.

Key

·	Bat contact, no score
X	Not played at
M	Played at and missed
1, 2, etc	Score/ball
W	Wicket

Other information could be noted. For example, OE might identify an outside edge of the bat or IE an inside edge.

Statistics
114 runs were scored off 23 overs.
3 wickets were lost.
Obviously other significant statistics can be highlighted, some of which refer to batting as against bowling.

In closing this chapter, there are one or two final 'nettles to grasp' which, whilst controversial, are an essential principle for all coaches to consider.

What is talent?
What is the measure of talent?
Should a coach take risks with talent?
What is good performance?
What is a better performance?
Is performance measured purely by results?
What is success? Is it maximising talent?
What is a good technique?
Is good technique measured by results?

51

These are difficult questions I know, but very relevant to my comments on the dangers of coaching (Chapter 1), and questions that need to be answered to some degree by the cricket coach.

In answering these and other questions that quickly come to mind, each coach must delve deep into his conscience. He must ask himself many questions in turn. Am I good enough to do this or that? If not why not? The coach must be absolutely honest in his view of the future. He must honestly answer the question: Is my involvement with this player to his benefit in twelve months' time? If the answer is an honest 'yes' then the coach must proceed and do his best considering, in the main, the serious ambitions of the player concerned. This factor above all others must be the guiding light. Therefore any programme for improving a player's performance must be *extremely carefully* compiled.

I can think of an outstanding example of the subject under discussion in Nick Faldo, the golfer. Nick's desire to achieve what *he thinks* to be his own ultimate performance (a thought supported by expert coaches) necessitated the smallest of swing changes. Small, yes, but major in that Nick's already successful swing had been well grooved for many years. Nick Faldo did, in fact, 'pick up his particular nettle' and I say 'more strength to his elbow'. At the time of writing, it looks as if he was right to do so.

Suppose he was wrong in terms of success; suppose any coach makes a mistake and contributes to a player's lack of success. Where do we go from there? Only back up again, because if you have genuinely done your best and worked it out with the player concerned there can be no recriminations. Neither he nor you could have been happy not trying!

SKILL ANALYSIS PHOTOGRAPHS

As noted earlier in this chapter, sequence photographs can be very useful in skill analysis. So can the single photograph, providing it is timed and taken very carefully. Examples of both sequence and single photographs are shown in bowling, batting and wicket-keeping.

Figs 39 to 44 show a sequence of Greg Thomas in action. Compare these with the five basic positions. From these photographs, I am optimistic that Greg will make a top class fast bowler. He has good technique. Developing the right attitude towards fitness and making a serious in-depth study of tactics should now be his main aim. His coach should also make sure that he is not overbowled in matches or in practice.

Figs 45 to 48 show examples from one of the two key positions in the bowling action, the 'coil', and Figs 49 to 52 show the follow-through, the other key position.

Bowling (Figs 38 to 52)

Fig 38 Four England bowlers – Les Taylor, Bob Willis, Neil Foster and coach Bob Cottam – watch a 'Press' demonstration by Greg Thomas from Glamorgan.

Fig 39 An excellent position 1. The twist of the front shoulder begins the 'coil', storing up the energy to be released into the delivery.

Fig 40 The 'coil' position. A pronounced 'lean away' from the batsman at just the right time. Everything is right!

Fig 41 Perfect delivery stride maintaining the 'sideways' position. An arched back stabilises this important position.

Fig 42 The 'spring' is released. The front leg landing in line with the back leg flexes slightly to take the full weight of the body through the delivery. The late unwinding of the body allows the arm to come through with maximum effect.

Fig 43 The magnificent head position throughout the action is maintained here in the beginning of the follow-through.

Fig 44 The follow-through is positive – straight down the wicket, again with the head leading, demonstrating what is undoubtedly a first-class bowling action.

Fig 45 Top half good – bottom half bad. This stiff legged position will restrict balance and in this case is obviously the beginning of a no-ball.

Fig 46 Might make an inswing bowler of medium pace – but this is not the action to model. It is difficult to see how real pace can be generated from this position. Remember, however, that coaching is to do with getting the best out of a player. Radical changes would be needed for this young man to achieve the classical action.

Fig 47 Nearly the perfect 'coil' position. There is a little stiffness here which may be cleared with a well-designed fitness programme.

Fig 48 Again a near perfect 'coil'. If this young man could land his right foot a little more parallel to the crease, I think it would give him a stronger body action and the possibility of bowling the away swinger. In spite of this, he has great potential.

Fig 49 No-ball! Apart from the open position and minimal use of the non bowling arm, the bowling of no-balls in practice is contagious and should be a main source of concern to both bowler and coach.

Fig 50 Almost a classical follow-through position: the bowler looking over the bowling shoulder at the batsman.

Fig 52 Magnificent – and so it should be! Neil Foster of Essex and England shows all the techniques of the high class fast bowler. Particularly notice the lean forward towards the batsman and the total effort that has gone into the delivery.

Fig 51 A big fault here, you cannot hit the target if you do not look at it.

56

Batting (Figs 53 to 56)

Fig 53 Who says boys do not copy Test players? A Graham Gooch in the making?

Fig 54 Peter Willey –a reasonably successful batsman at the highest level, with a stance I find difficult to recommend.

Fig 55 This looks more like it! Allan Lamb's stance here I do find easy to recommend.

Fig 56 No matter what your stance, if you play strokes like this I cannot fancy your chances as a batsman. This is the well-known 'cross bat slog'. Whatever anyone says, the best batsmen play strokes with a straight bat most of the time, whether the straight bat be horizontal or vertical.

Wicket-keeping (Figs 57 & 58)

Fig 57 So far so good!

COMMON FAULTS IN BATTING AND BOWLING

Batting

Assume that players are right-handed unless stated otherwise.

GRIP

1. Hands too far apart on the bat handle – restricts stroke play.
2. Bottom hand too low on the bat handle – prevents straight bat play.
3. Left wrist too far behind the handle restricts follow-through.
4. Left wrist too far in front of the handle reduces control.
5. Too strong a grip with bottom hand, too weak a grip with top hand.

STANCE

1. Feet too far apart – restricts movement.

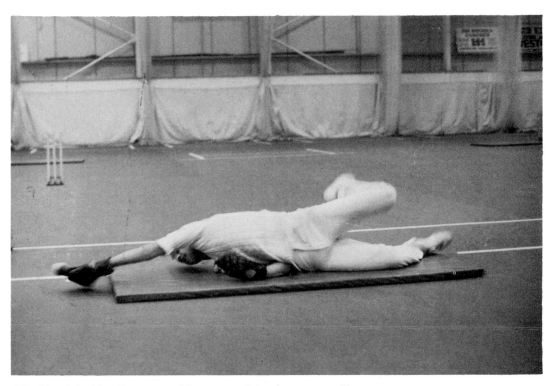

Fig 58 A bad landing causes this young wicket-keeper to spill the catch. Look to turn the landing shoulder 'under and up' to break the fall and protect the catch. This is great practice for keepers. Note the crash mat.

2. Feet too close together – causes loss of balance.

3. 'Open' stance (chest facing bowler) prevents straight backlift and causes excessive body movement in off-side play.

4. Eyes not level.

5. Head not turned fully towards the bowler – restricts view of delivery.

6. Head not in line with middle stump.

7. Head well over towards off-side causes loss of balance – a very common fault.

BACKLIFT

1. Cramped front elbow – reduces length of backlift and reduces power.

2. Not 'opening' bat face towards point – tends to shut bat face in downswing.

3. Late pick-up.

BACK DEFENCE

1. Not stepping far enough back, with back foot parallel to the crease – thus keeping the body sideways.
2. Not taking the front shoulder and consequently the back foot far enough towards the line of the ball.
3. Not keeping the backlift straight enough.
4. Not keeping the balance of the head and body forward towards the line of the ball on contact.
5. Not keeping control of the bat with the top hand.
6. Not keeping the front elbow high enough.

BACK ATTACK: PULL STROKE

1. Not moving early enough behind the line of the ball.
2. Restricting the backlift.
3. Not attempting to hit the ball at arm's length.
4. Trying to hit the ball behind square leg rather than in front.
5. Hitting too hard – and not watching the ball properly.
6. Not keeping the balance of the body forward.

BACK ATTACK: SQUARE CUT

1. Moving away from the line of the ball.
2. Not lifting the bat high enough.
3. Not staying sideways (i.e. back foot parallel to crease) when playing the stroke.
4. Playing the stroke too close to the body, cramping the arms.
5. Not transferring the weight fully on to the back foot.

BACK ATTACK: FORCING SHOT

1. Not making the movements for the back defence – but with a longer and higher backlift.
2. Not having the intention to hit the ball hard.
3. Not keeping the bat face on the line of the stroke.

FORWARD DEFENCE

1. Not leading with the left shoulder and head towards the line of the ball – *this applies to every stroke in batting.*
2. Not taking the front foot forward enough just inside the line of the ball, allowing the back leg a full stretch.
3. Not bending the front knee – to 'close the gate'.
4. Not angling the bat handle forward to keep the ball down.
5. Not restricting the forward movement of the bat on contact.
6. Not controlling the bat with the top hand.
7. Controlling the bat with the bottom hand and allowing the bat face to close.
8. Not keeping the inside of the back foot grounded – behind the crease.

FORWARD ATTACK: THE DRIVES

All the points noted for forward defence apply except the following:

1. Not allowing a longer backlift with minimum bending of the front elbow.
2. Not having the intention of hitting the ball hard enough.
3. Not looking for the longest possible follow-through with the hands high. This applies to both the full and check drives.

Note When moving down the wicket to drive, the main fault is in not having the confidence to move quickly 'all the way'. Once there you can always play defensively if not quite in the right position.

FORWARD ATTACK: THE SWEEP

1. Not selecting the correct ball to sweep – that is, trying to sweep the over pitched ball rather than the good length ball pitched outside the leg stump.
2. Not having the front pad in the line between the path of the ball and the stumps.
3. Trying to hit the ball with arms cramped.

Bowling

1. Incorrect grip for the delivery intended.
2. Not having a rhythmic and accelerating run-up.
3. Having too long or too short a run-up for your physique and type of bowling.
4. Not gathering yourself mentally and physically just before you 'bound' into the delivery stride.
5. Not 'bounding' from the left foot with the height and shoulder rotation to land in the delivery stride with the right foot parallel to the crease.
6. An insufficient arch of the back and lean away from the batsman when landing in the delivery stride.
7. Too long or too short a delivery stride – either can cause fundamental errors.
8. Not looking down the wicket from behind a high front arm.
9. Front foot splaying wide in the delivery stride.
10. Poor use of the front arm throughout the delivery and follow-through.
11. An incomplete and weak follow-through.
12. Poor concentration and no planning of each delivery.

Fig 59 Ian Botham (England)

6 Planning and Course Design

If there is one aspect of coaching in which we can all improve, it must be in *planning*. That is not to say we do not plan our coaching now, we do, but in recent years there have been marvellous innovations in this field, and I doubt whether coaches in general have really made any special effort to introduce them into their own coaching programmes. Finance may be a reason for this, although it need not be unless one is thinking in terms of computers and so on. I am tempted to think that the coach, and particularly the involved amateur coach, has so little time and so much to do that the physical aspect of coaching tends to become a priority. Even so, I put forward the view that if we just took time to look a little longer at the possibilities, we would find that spending more time on planning would pay handsome dividends in terms of success.

One of the coach's problems has always been in planning the efficient use of available coaching time. One's thinking, instead of looking at a broader planning base, tends to be short term: planning for today, in fact, or maybe tomorrow or for the next week, and that's all. Let me suggest that we re-examine our coaching strategy. Deliberately make thinking time available to set short, medium and long-term plans, all incorporated in a master plan which is itself well monitored and as a consequence periodically updated to serve its purpose properly. There is no doubt about it, a little extra thought and effort will produce the most gratifying results and real appreciation from everyone concerned, not least the players who are being coached. If you are like me, the feeling of being well organised, if only occasionally, is certainly a good one.

COACHING COURSES

Well-organised coaching courses have been progressively attracting more enthusiastic young cricketers in recent years and in many ways have contributed to the upsurge in coaching and competition in junior and youth cricket. Of course, the variety and excitement of international cricket on the television has put the 'icing on the cake', but one without the other would leave an unbridgeable gap I am sure. It is, indeed, a healthy situation requiring an equally healthy attitude and response from coaches and their associations. Courses and techniques of coaching will need to be presented with increasing thoughtfulness. Syllabuses and course designs will need to be progressive and interesting to withstand the inevitable challenge from other sports for the attentions of our young people.

Let us take a look at coaching courses in general. Presented in different forms, invariably they are likely to be a series of sessions, each planned independently but giving a continuity to the course as a whole that will ensure a lasting benefit to those that attend. This sounds fine, but whilst a session can be very well planned in itself, it is still essential to ensure that one session joins naturally with the next to cover the syllabus and give the participants a feeling for the course as a whole rather than an isolated session.

'One swallow doesn't make a summer', and the coach who is running the course must be very much aware of this. One bad lecture, one bad practice session, one 'mess-up' in a film show – all the result of bad planning, could ruin months of otherwise excellent preparation. Coaches take heed, it happens all the time – more than you would ever think and to all of us at some time. Next time try not to let it happen to you!

Obviously readers will appreciate, without the foregoing comment, that a good knowledge of course design and planning in all its forms is one of the most important attributes of the good coach. I repeat, time invested in this area of coaching is certain to pay off. For example, remember the importance of the course syllabus. On the face of it a syllabus is simply a list of topics covered on a course. It is important, even *vital*, to the coach to assess the course syllabus in *detail* if he is to be properly prepared.

COURSE DESIGN AND ORGANISATION

* The first requirement is to establish whether or not there is a need for a course.

This should be a success story – the problem is to find out the maximum numbers that will be interested not the minimum! This will be achieved by maximum publicity within the catchment area, in clubs, schools or whatever organisations are likely to produce participants on the course. Various forms of enquiry will reveal the potential: i.e. meetings between interested parties, not fogetting parents, but in general coaching associations, cricket club officials (county and local), sports centre officials, teachers' groups and education authorities. Newspapers, magazines or suitably designed and located posters will pose the questions as will well-written circulars from the course organisers to the likely sources of interest.

Having thoroughly reviewed the potential and agreed to proceed, a number of decisions need to be made fairly quickly.

1. What is the age group concerned?
2. How many in this age group can be properly catered for?
3. Will it be an outdoor or an indoor activity? This will depend upon the time of the year and the facilities available.
4. Is the course to be of a general or specialised nature? That is, for batsmen only, or open to bowlers only, or skill assessment and so on.
5. Will the coaches required be available on the dates envisaged, are they qualified and what will they cost?
6. Will the facilities and equipment be available on the dates envisaged and what will they cost?
7. Have grant possibilities been fully investigated? The earlier this can be done the better.
8. Is the course budget realistic and can a proper fee for each participant be set?
9. Having obtained the answers to

these questions, is the course still viable? 10. If the answer is yes, application forms will need to be produced and circulated, whilst the course organisers and the coaches concerned (maybe one and the same) will need to finalise the course design noting its particular requirements in terms of the back-up services.

If the time, place and number of sessions have been decided, the finishing touches can be put to the course programme. Final numbers of participants will have been agreed upon, preferably with a view to the balance of the course and the facilities available, i.e. even numbers are better than odd, multiples of four are good. Nothing is worse than young cricketers coming to a course that turns out to be a shambles because of bad organisation. The best coaches in the world cannot make up for a slipshod set-up.

Once all the participants are registered and their fees have been paid, everything is ready. Everyone – organisations, coaches, participants – is keen. From now on the pressure is on the coach – or should be. Each session should be approached as a continuation of the last one even though it is important in its own right. The longer the course goes on, the more important it will be for the coach to prepare his material and rekindle his enthusiasm. Some coaches may not think so – but if they don't, they are taking a chance and I am afraid that cannot be a coach's prerogative. The last session must, if anything, be better than the first.

Planning the Sessions

Having commented already on the importance of good course design and the careful planning of each session, we can now look at the requirements a little closer. No coach worth his salt will go into a coaching session without having thought very seriously about what he is going to say and do. That much is owed to those who attend. Obviously some sort of written preparation is essential if the session is to be as successful as possible – even if it is just a series of headings to act as reminders. *Fail to prepare – Prepare to fail*: this is a truism in coaching if ever there was one. In making a written preparation, not only will you record your intentions in some way, but as soon as you put pen to paper you will question your intentions and as a result *improve* them, to everyone's benefit. Thorough preparation does work! Your ideas can then be discussed that much more easily with colleagues, resulting in new ideas from them, which in themselves will stimulate the group and multiply progress.

The well-known formula for the coaching or practice session is worth recording here, with examples that may well be used by coaches in clubs and schools.

The main aim of the session should be to introduce, revise or improve a particular skill and should occupy an early part of the total available period. This should be divided as follows, whenever possible, to add variety:

1. A warm-up.
2. A main skill to practise or learn.
3. A competitive cricket game.

WARM-UP

Warm-up activities should be vigorous, to stimulate the players and capture their interest. The quality of any subsequent practice depends upon the involvement and concentration established in this period. Many fielding activities and minor games (for example chasing and retrieving, attacking fielding in pairs, dodge ball and so on) come into this category.

MAIN SKILL TRAINING

The main part of the session *may* consist of two parts. The first is the revision of a known skill. The second may be the teaching of a completely new skill or it may be a continuation of the skill that was revised. Very often in a net session it is a concentrated effort between player and coach on improving one small facet of a skill.

COMPETITION

This activity, depending upon the time and space available, may be a competition for points based on the skills taught, i.e. practice for the Proficiency Award Tests. Alternatively one of the cricket games described in Chapter 9 can provide an enjoyable and worthwhile finish. In competition players invariably come under pressure and in doing so a really good test of the skills taught is provided.

Depending upon the time, facilities, number and abilities of the youngsters, so the session must be planned.

School Games Lesson

The teacher will have minimum time (one hour maximum) and perhaps forty children. With this situation the main aim of the lesson will have to be achieved through group coaching methods, as it would if large numbers were involved in a club practice night. If the class is very young and inexperienced, groups will generally practise the same skill as it is taught, before moving on to the competition. Groups of older and more experienced children will be able to practise not only the skill taught but other skills too, for example one group may practise bowling from the 'coil' position, another the off-drive and so on. Changing the skills gives variety within the period available.

Club or School Team Practice Session

When cricket nets and a ground are available, numbers and time are not always so critical and a different approach can be planned. A warm-up is always necessary and whenever possible one should try to finish with a competition. However, the main skill will take a different form as individual net coaching can be organised. If the numbers are such that they cannot all be accommodated in the nets, group coaching sequences can be undertaken outside the net. In fact, even when nets are available for all, a group coaching session can be well worth while.

Typical School Games Lesson Plan (For Younger Children)

Number in class: 30
Age: under 11
Duration of lesson: 45 minutes
Aim: to teach the forward drive.

WARM-UP

Five minutes. Chasing and throwing, working in pairs using a chair as a wicket.
1. Player One rolls, Player Two chases at full speed, picks up and returns.
2. Player One takes the return, Player Two trots back to the wicket.

They have five turns each, and change round.

Coaching points
1. Five times pick up off right foot, pivot and throw.
2. Five times pick up off left foot, pivot, step and throw.

MAIN SKILL

Twenty-five minutes. Forward drive to straight ball.

1. Arrange the class in two rows, left-handers together at right-hand end of rows.
2. Demonstrate facing the same direction as the class at the correct speed, describing the type of delivery to which stroke is played.

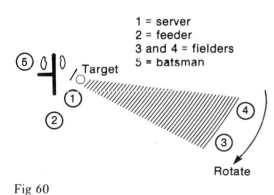

1 = server
2 = feeder
3 and 4 = fielders
5 = batsman

Target

Rotate

Fig 60

3. Class mirror the stroke at the correct speed – give individual correction.
4. Select a group of five. Arrange the group onto previously fixed markings (Fig 60).
5. Drop ball – batsman drives on second bounce. Fielders retrieve and ball is returned to feeder. Repeat (group has several balls).
6. Divide the class into groups of five and begin the practice. Emphasise organisation, not technique. Change batsman in turn.
7. Once every player has had a turn, demonstrate again, emphasising one or two main points in technique.
8. Players continue the practice. Give individual coaching and comment on any general faults.

Coaching points
1. Pick up bat before ball is released.
2. Foot to ball.
3. Strike on second half volley.
4. Bat follows through in the direction the ball has been struck.
5. Keep the head down and still.

COMPETITION

Fifteen minutes. Scoring runs with forward drive. Markings adapted and skittles set out (Fig 61).

Rules
1. General organisation as before.
2. Ten strokes each unless run out or caught out.
3. Ball must be struck on ground between skittles A and B – for this, one run is scored.
4. If ball is correctly struck, batsman may run to score additional runs. One run is scored if batsman reaches skittle C,

two runs if he gets back to his own crease, and so on.

5. A batsman can be run out at the end to which he is running, in which case his innings is closed.

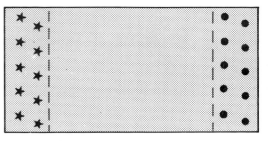

Fig 62

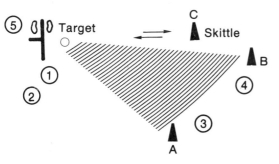

Fig 61

Typical School or Club Group Practice Lesson Plan (For Older Children)

Number in class: 30
Age: over 11
Duration of lesson: one and a half hours
Aim: to introduce the skill of bowling the off-spinner.

WARM-UP

Ten minutes. Activity: fielding competition.

1. Pair children off and send to appropriate end of court (Fig 62).
2. Each team has to skim or roll the ball on the ground. To score a point, the players in team one have to get the ball over team two's back line and vice versa.
3. Start by using one tennis ball and as the game progresses introduce more balls until there are up to ten in play.

MAIN SKILL

Thirty minutes. Off-spin bowling.

1. In pairs, each player has a rubber ball with seam chalked on. Demonstrate grip and spinning action underhand.
2. Players practise this underhand individually, then: in pairs underhand; in pairs throwing; in pairs bowling, short distance and moving back to approximately twenty yards.

Coaching points
1. Seam at right angles to axis of hand.
2. Forefinger bent along the seam – ball spun from first joint of forefinger.
3. Turn wrist in clockwise direction and flick with fingers at the same time.
4. Obtain maximum spin; cultivate direction later.

Thirty minutes. Divide into three groups of ten: A, B and C. Ten minute changes.
A – Continue to practise off-spin, using a chair as wicket.
B – Subdivide into two groups of five. Each group practises backfoot attack as already taught, changing round every ten balls (Fig 63).
C – Subdivide into two groups of five. Each group practises slip catching (*see* Chapter 9).

COMPETITION

Twenty-five minutes. Within groups A, B and C, finish with a game of continuous cricket – five-a-side. Rules as before except: change the bowler every six balls, and the bowler must bowl underhand off-spinners, which bounce only once. Any ball delivered otherwise counts as a no-ball, giving one run to the other side.

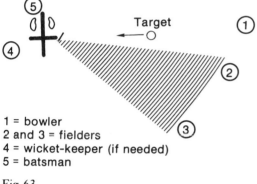

1 = bowler
2 and 3 = fielders
4 = wicket-keeper (if needed)
5 = batsman

Fig 63

Typical Club or School Team Practice Session Plan

Number in squad: up to 16
Age: 14 upwards
Duration of session: two and a half hours

WARM-UP

Fifteen minutes. Attacking fielding and long catching.

1. Work in pairs, using one stump as wicket. One player acts as wicket-keeper and rolls the ball to his partner running in from about twenty-five to thirty yards. Repeat a number of times and change over.

2. Practise throwing, hitting and catching from up to thirty yards.

MAIN SKILL

Up to one and a half hours. Concentrate on improving one or more individual batting and/or bowling skills, in net practice and in a group coaching situation, if necessary.

1. Allow no more than six players per net. Up to twenty minutes batting per player.
2. If only one net is available, group coaching sequences on individual skills can be arranged.

Note Whenever possible, give all players batting coaching in nets, but when time is limited, ensure that the better bowlers bowl at the better batsmen.

COMPETITION

Up to one hour. A six- or eight-a-side game (*see* Chapter 9) if a good wicket is available.

FACTORS IN COURSE DESIGN

As mentioned previously, it is very important when designing a course to take into consideration the age group of the players attending. Very often fairly loose headings are put on to courses, giving little indication of their content. For example general coaching can be given to under nineteen year olds, that would be more suitable for under fourteens. Conversely, special skills sessions can be given to under fourteens when, in fact,

COACH'S REPORT

Player | **Course Details**

Name: Name:
Address: Venue:
                                           Dates:

Telephone Number: Coach i/c:
Date of Birth: Address:
Club/School:
Recommended by: Telephone Number:

Cricket Background:

Main Assets:

Main Faults:

Coach's Comments:

Signed: ....   Date: ....

Fig 64

they are unsuitable and should be aimed at, say, under nineteens. Course literature should clearly state the age group it is meant for.

Inherent in any good coaching course is realistic and full monitoring of the players on the course. Only from detailed reports, in whatever form, can proper continuity of coaching take place. Fig 64 shows an example of a typical coach's report. I consider poor monitoring and recording of performance (analysis) to be the biggest drawback in the development of players over the years. I wonder just how many players have not reached anywhere near their potential simply because their *names* have not been passed on to the appropriate authority, let alone a record of their true ability!

SETTING OF GOALS

This subject could be included in most chapters of this book as goal setting can be a means of stimulating or motivating *both player and coach*. For the player, match play can be fairly straightforward by simply setting targets in terms of figures. However, this can be very misleading as it does not take into consideration the opposition, the conditions of play, and so on. In practice sessions or on a course, goal setting can be very specific with the use of a video-recorder. Like with like can be very definitely compared and the achievement or otherwise of a set goal positively identified. Taking this principle further, the enthusiastic player/coach partnership can introduce the principle with all the plans they have – short, mid and long term. I am a great believer in setting as many realistic and interesting goals as possible. Effort is the spur and fifty per cent of one hundred is fifty; fifty per cent of zero is still zero!

One of the best examples of goal setting I have seen and experienced in coaching is the National Cricket Association's Proficiency Award Scheme. It is ideal for encouraging young cricketers between nine and fifteen years of age, setting testing but achievable targets. The scheme is, in effect, measured group coaching and fits well into most coaching courses for the under thirteen age group particularly. It can also be a measure

of coaching ability, a point worth remembering for coaches who want to consider some sort of self-examination of their progress.

Prevention of Injury on Courses

Young cricketers these days seem to suffer an increasing number of injuries. I am sure that various reasons will be put forward for this. Personally I am impressed by research recently undertaken in this field both in England and Australia. I am thinking particularly of work done and lectures I have attended by Bernard Thomas, one of England's leading sports physiotherapists, better known for his long-standing service with the England team. Clive Bond, Head of Carnegie School of Physical Education and Human Movement Studies, has instituted research programmes that can be of enormous benefit to cricket. Darryl Foster, West Australian cricket coach and physical educationalist, and my great friend and former colleague, Frank Tyson of Victoria, Australia, seem to be advancing just as rapidly and are just as concerned as we are in Britain.

The willingness of a unique variety of experts in different fields of medicine to co-operate with such men, throws a new light on the physical training of cricketers. This is why in planning courses, coaches need to be aware of the most recent progress. For example, opinions from these areas of research indicate that real harm can be done by young fast bowlers trying to bowl *too fast for too long*. As a result, proper guidelines from informed authorities are being made available for coaches to include in their course planning.

FAST BOWLING GUIDELINES

Age Group	Match	Practice
Under 12	A limit of two spells of four overs with approximately a one-hour break.	Two thirty-minute practice sessions per week. Five-minute short run – reduced pace. Twenty-minute match speed – coach controlled. Five-minute specific technique development.
Under 16	A limit of two spells of six overs with approximately a one-hour break.	Two forty-minute practice sessions per week. Five-minute short run – reduced pace. Twenty-five minute match speed – coach controlled. Ten-minute specific technique development.
Under 19	A limit of three spells of six overs with approximately a one-hour break.	Three forty-minute practice sessions per week. Five-minute short run – reduced pace. Twenty-five minute match speed – coach controlled. Ten-minute specific technique development.
Seniors	A limit of three spells of eight overs with approximately a one-hour break.	Three one-hour practice sessions per week. Ten-minute short run – reduced pace. Forty-minute match speed – coach controlled. Ten-minute specific technique.

PAIN

It is essential that the player and coach accept pain as a warning, which if ignored may lead to an injury that could ruin a career. The young growing cricketer is particularly vulnerable. If soreness develops, the player should ease off or stop for a few days. Persistent pain should be investigated by a doctor and will probably require treatment from a physiotherapist.

Booking of Facilities

One of the most frustrating aspects of coaching course design and organisation is in the booking of suitable accommodation for the particular course one has in mind. I have had one or two embarrassing lessons in this field of planning. By leaving the booking of facilities too late it is easy to become very exposed to frustration and valid criticism. It sounds a fairly simple exercise to book a sports hall or a few rooms for overnight accommodation and there is a temptation to sort out the other problems of the operation first. *Never make this mistake.* Before you do anything else of significance in your course planning, *check* whether or not you can obtain the facilities you are likely to need. Only when you have confirmed this can you really go ahead with confidence.

Good facilities with suitable accommodation are becoming more and more difficult to obtain as coaches and their associations (in all sports) require them to achieve their aims. *You have been warned!*

Finance

Setting up coaching courses, competitions and so on requires two vital ingredients – people and money. This book assumes to some degree that the coach will not be completely alone and may be part of an association of people, whatever they may call themselves. Finance for coaching is a different matter. Anyone connected with cricket will know that whilst equipment and clothing is very expensive, club membership is very cheap compared to other sports and pastimes. The financing of coaching courses is, therefore, a problem as there is a tendency to think that coaching goes along with club membership, which is not necessarily the case. There are, however, many agencies from which finance for coaching can be obtained, although it is not the object of this book to be a directory of financial resources for coaching.

Those with the responsibility for coaching should, as in the case of checking on facilities, make *early* enquiries into the financing of projects in hand. Grant Aid is the biggest source of direct finance to coaching and this may come from official cricketing associations, local, county, regional or national, depending upon the catchment area from which the young cricketers will attend the project. Local education or council authorities may be approached. Clubs themselves are usually well prepared to finance junior cricket ventures through running some form of cash raising event – film shows, proficiency awards and so on. Sponsorship plays a major role these days, but strangely enough parents are not the sources of paying for their children's cricket education that they might be. This is not a criticism of parents, I think it is simply because they are not approached. With all the sources of finance available however, perhaps it is not such a problem, providing that the enterprise, coaching course or whatever, is *well organised*. That is, a good, well-presented programme conducted in uncramped facilities with well-maintained playing conditions, under the guidance of qualified and enthusiastic coaches. In other words, a *totally well-planned operation*, with interesting and worthwhile feedback to all who have contributed. Everyone appreciates value for money!

Finally, planners, bear in mind the simple things: the year planner, the filing system (that works), the address book of *all* possible contacts (you will need them) complete with telephone numbers, and don't forget, the coach's life-saver – the pocket diary.

UNDER FOURTEEN RESIDENTIAL COURSE

Dear

We are pleased to invite you to the above course which will be held at
the County Indoor Cricket School, and we are pleased to record our
appreciation to — Cricket Club for allowing us to use the indoor
school.

The course is structured to provide enjoyable and instructive sessions.
All aspects of the game, batting, bowling, wicket-keeping and fielding,
are covered, together with discussions on captaincy, the laws and cricket
etiquette.

Coaching slides and films, plus the use of a video camera/recorder
provide valuable coaching aids to support our very fine team of
experienced and fully qualified coaches.

I do hope you can attend and look forward to meeting you.

Best wishes

Course:
Date:
Reception: 9.00 a.m. at the indoor school
Venue: Accommodation:

                            Coaching:

Dress: Students are reminded that white cricket clothing including indoor
                            footwear must be worn at all coaching sessions.
                            Jackets and ties must be worn at dinner.
Coaching staff: Four well qualified coaches:
Evening supervision: Two coaches will reside with the students.
Fee: The fee is £... and this must be paid before ...
                            Cheques payable to ...
Parents: Parents are very welcome to view the sessions. Meals and drinks can b
                            obtained from the pavilion bar.
Equipment: Students are advised to bring their own bat, pads, gloves and a leathe
                            cricket ball.

Fig 65   The letter in this typical course correspondence gives
         useful information, to which other information, such as
         recommended course literature, reply forms etc. can be
         added. For difficult venues a basic map and directions can
         also be included. More information is better than less.
         The coach in charge must have seen the proposed time-
         table in good time, so that lesson plans and necessary
         equipment can be made available.

Course Timetable

Thursday

9.00 a.m.	Reception	Indoor school
9.30 a.m.	Warm-up	Indoor school
	Batting skills (front foot play)	Indoor school
10.15 a.m.	Net session/slides	Indoor school
11.15 a.m.	Morning break	Pavilion
11.30 a.m.	Net session/slides/films	Indoor school
12.30 p.m.	Luncheon interval	Pavilion
1.30 p.m.	Batting skills (back foot play)	Indoor school
2.15 p.m.	Net session/video	Indoor school/pavilion
3.15 p.m.	Afternoon break	Pavilion
3.30 p.m.	Net session/video	Indoor school/pavilion
4.15 p.m.	Departure by mini bus	
6.30 p.m.	Dinner	Dining-room
7.45 p.m.	Film/quiz/entertainment	Lounge
9.00 p.m.	Indoor soccer/table sports	Sports hall
9.45 p.m.	Free time	
10.30 p.m.	Retire to own room	
10.45 p.m.	Lights out	

Friday

8.00 a.m.	Breakfast	Dining-room
8.45 a.m.	Departure by mini bus (dress: cricket clothing & full kit)	Assemble main entrance
9.00 a.m.	Warm-up	Indoor school
9.30 a.m.	Bowling skills	Indoor school
10.00 a.m.	Net session/video	Indoor school/pavilion
11.00 a.m.	Morning break	
11.15 a.m.	Bowling skills (spin)	Indoor school
11.45 a.m.	Net session/video	Indoor school/pavilion
12.45 p.m.	Luncheon interval	Pavilion
1.45 p.m.	Fielding and wicket-keeping skills	Indoor school
2.30 p.m.	Net session/video	Indoor school/pavilion
3.15 p.m.	Afternoon break	Pavilion
3.30 p.m.	Net session/video	Indoor school/pavilion
4.15 p.m.	Course tournament	Indoor school
5.15 p.m.	End of course: summary and depart	Indoor school

Fig 66   Jeffrey Dujon (West Indies)

7 Teaching for Coaches

As highlighted in Chapter 1, the ability to *teach* the skills of cricket is of paramount importance in the repertoire of the good cricket coach. This seems a fairly obvious statement, but in some cricket coaching circles the special skills of teaching are not recognised as being quite so important. It is felt by some that the skills of teaching come naturally and so do not necessarily require special instruction. This may be so for the odd 'genius', but I am sure that for the great majority the more special knowledge and skill that can be acquired to do the job in hand, the better the job will be done. Learning is a difficult enough process as it is, without restricting its potential.

If coaches expect young cricketers to take instruction and learn from them, it is logical and realistic that coaches themselves can learn from instruction relevant to *their* role. Communication in all its forms is very much the key factor. This is not to say that the cricket coach needs a degree in education, or anything like it, to acquire skills of teaching that would be of sound practical value. Far from it, but by attending special ancillary courses

Fig 67   Even Test batsmen need checking from time to time. Coaches Graham Saville and Doug Ferguson check Pakistan Test batsman Wasim Raja on the defensive back stroke. Student coaches look on.

designed to suit the coach and by sensible reading of the subject, there is not the slightest doubt that an improvement in overall coaching ability would follow. If coaching is to have any credibility and if cricket coaches are to have any real status in cricket and society (not to mention sport in general) it is a principle to be followed.

THE PRINCIPLES OF LEARNING

1. The coach should clearly state what a player should know and be able to do at the end of a period of instruction. For example, after completing a course on the basics of batting, a player should know the principles of straight bat play, through grip, stance, backlift and shoulder/head lead. He should be able to apply these principles in the main forward and back strokes, to a reasonable degree, depending upon the amount of practice time undertaken.

2. The skills and techniques to be learned should be relevant to the aims and objectives of the course of instruction.

3. Instruction should be organised in short progressive steps in a sequence that is determined by each player's needs.

4. Instruction should be graded in difficulty so that players make few mistakes. The coach should organise *for success* and *minimise failure*.

5. Each player should be coached to suit his own pace of learning.

6. Players should be actively involved in all stages of the coach's instruction. They should know *why* the coach requires this or that to be done – or not done.

7. Players should receive continuous information on their individual progress throughout a course of instruction.

8. Each player should master each coaching point made, before beginning to concentrate on the next. To do this the player needs: a motive; time to take in the point in question; and the capacity to retain what has been taught. This is not always conducive to coaching in groups.

The experienced coach will have collected a library of information on cricket coaching – even if some of the 'library' is in his memory! He should periodically update his library and, if necessary, re-learn some of the material. Almost certainly some favourite material will have to be discarded.

The good coach will always make a point of identifying priorities.

LEARNING A SKILL

Many skills can be very lcearly demonstrated. Movements within a skill can be observed by the player, but he needs to be given hints (coaching points) and clues within the performance of the skill. Visual aids and verbal guidance are needed to supplement the demonstration. The *amount* of guidance given is important, but equally important is *when* the guidance is given, which is generally as soon as possible within the particular practice sequence.

Statement

Unless the elementary principles of specific skills (i.e. basic bowling action, hitting a ball to leg, catching etc) are experienced well before the age of fifteen, it is unlikely that they will be easily established and retained later.

A player's progress in the acquiring of a skill will vary both with the type and complexity of the skill and the capability of the player. However the sequence of learning a skill does form a definite pattern, broadly shown in Fig 68. A simple analysis of this graph will help both coach and player to understand the problems that lie ahead and give them the opportunity of preparing accordingly.

Comments on Learning a Skill

1. Progress is never constant.
2. Good teaching will produce outstanding early progress.
3. As skill is progressively acquired, further improvement takes considerably longer.
4. Periods of minimal or even no improvement can be anticipated.
5. Early success is *not* a guarantee of final success.
6. Different skills curves do not necessarily follow the same pattern for the same individual.

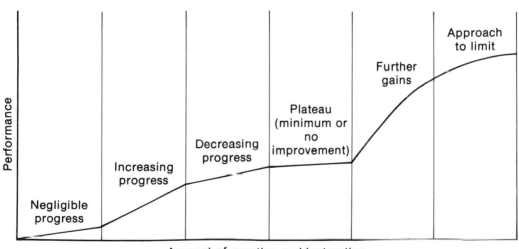

Fig 68   General learning curve

Plateau Periods

The plateau (no improvement) periods are of particular significance in coaching and can be caused by:

* A natural part of the learning process.
* Loss of interest.
* Loss of confidence.
* Bad coaching.

The following are some important factors relating to plateau periods for a coach to consider.

1. Too much fault finding results in loss of confidence.
2. Too early an introduction into competition can restrict progress.
3. A coach can be *too keen* for continually rapid progress. The player needs to enjoy new experiences before leaving them. If progress is not planned properly, the player can quickly lose interest.

Good Coaching Habits

The significant conclusions of research into the learning of a skill is the need for the coach to space practice time very carefully with the object of minimising plateaux (periods of minimal improvement). This is accomplished by developing good coaching habits; these include:

* Encouragement.
* Compassion.
* A sense of humour.
* Enthusiasm.
* Obvious technical expertise.
* Good demonstrations.
* Patience.
* In-depth planning.
* Self-criticism.

THE ART OF A GOOD COACH

1. To set a task that the *player* thinks is within his capacity. A player will tend not to attempt a task he feels is too difficult. Neither will he really apply himself to a task which is too easy. An even chance of success is usually the best motivator.
2. When possible, give players the opportunity of setting their own goals – providing they are not too easily attainable.
3. Recognise that players like to measure success. This is a point worth remembering, but worth even more in terms of motivation towards future targets is the allowing of time to enjoy the pleasure of the achievement of the last target. After a major target has been achieved, it is sound practice to set a number of smaller targets (or goals) taking less time.

TEACHING CRICKET SKILLS

The following routine is suggested for introducing a new skill.

Arrange the group so that everyone can see and hear and has sufficient room to perform the skill being taught.

1. Demonstrate and explain the purpose of the skill – all watch.
2. The group perform the skill – coach watches.
3. Coach comments and gives individual correction, whilst others continue to practise.
4. Coach gives general points of correction to whole group – all listen.

This initial introduction should be followed by:

5. Further demonstration, either by coach or by an accomplished member of the group.

6. Further practice by group – coach watches.

7. Coach highlights individual and general points.

This sequence should be repeated as often as is necessary, but each extra demonstration and practice should add something to the experience of the group. All practice must be commented upon and in as encouraging a way as possible.

Hints on Teaching Technique

1. Initial demonstration – give one or two indications of what to look for. The demonstration should be:
   (a) Performed at correct speed.
   (b) In the same direction as the group will perform.
   (c) Given with explanation of purpose of skill. Technical points should be kept to a minimum.
   (d) No more than one minute long.

2. The first practice should be the whole skill performed at correct speed. At this stage skills should not be broken down into component parts.

3. Individual coaching, during practice, should be done in a manner audible to the whole group, since most of them will be making similar mistakes.

4. General comments should be simple and only cover the coaching points already given. Comments should be as encouraging as possible.

5. Further demonstration should emphasise the following:

   (a) Correct starting and finishing position of the skill.
   (b) The whole skill should be demonstrated.
   (c) Only a few key coaching points should be given.

6. During practice everyone should be encouraged to check the coaching points themselves, especially correct starting and finishing positions.

7. If necessary, general comments might now emphasise the part of the skill with which most of the group are having difficulty. Further practice might emphasise this part and lead to an isolated practice, but it must soon be put back into the whole skill pattern, so that there is always a sequence of whole–part–whole. A part practice can be shadowing the stroke without a ball, to improve the 'shape' of the stroke with the whole group.

Sample Introductory Course for the Teaching of Cricket

The aims of the course are to give men and women who are concerned with the education and welfare of children (of school age) a basic knowledge of cricket instruction. This type of course can also be used by coaches/teachers to teach children the basic skills of cricket.

Note By doubling or trebling the times suggested, the skills can be assimilated that much more.

SESSION ONE (ONE HOUR)

1. (Fifteen minutes) *Warm-up* – fielding; intercepting.

2. (Forty-five minutes) *Main skill* – batting.
   (a) The pull stroke, demonstrating the principles of group coaching.

(b) Grip, stance and backlift.

(c) Forward defence.

SESSION TWO (ONE HOUR)

3. (Fifty minutes) *Main skill* – bowling.
   (a) Brief talk on the bowling action.
   (b) The 'coil' – instruction.
   (c) The 'bound' – instruction.
   (d) The complete action – instruction.
4. (Ten minutes) *Final activity* – game. Continuous cricket.

SESSION THREE (ONE HOUR)

5. (Fifteen minutes) *Warm-up* – fielding.
   (a) Retrieving.
   (b) Catching.
6. (Thirty minutes) *Main skill* – batting.
   (a) Back defence.
   (b) Drives off the front foot.
7. (Fifteen minutes) *Final activity* – bowling. Practice bowling at targets/stumps.

SESSION FOUR (ONE HOUR)

8. (Fifteen minutes) *Warm-up* – fielding.
   (a) Long barrier and quick revision of retrieving.
   (b) Catching – skim catch and over the shoulder catch.
9. (Forty-five minutes) *Main theme* – group practice lesson.
   (a) The pull stroke.
   (b) Bowling at target/stumps.
   (c) Off-drive.
   (d) Intercepting – returns to wicket-keeper.

SESSION FIVE (ONE HOUR)

10. (One hour) *Introduction* – Proficiency Award Scheme. Instruction in setting up the total scheme, plus:
    (a) One bowling test – complete.
    (b) One batting test – complete.
    (c) One fielding test – complete.

SESSION SIX (ONE HOUR)

11. (One hour) *Practice* – games. Mini-cricket (*see* Chapter 9) and similar.

Other Aspects of Teaching Cricket

The subject of planning for coaches has been dealt with in Chapter 6, but there are a number of aspects of the coach's work relating to planning that seem to be appropriate to this chapter. In particular there is the *syllabus*, which is simply a list of topics covered by a course. Once a course has been designed it will be necessary to publish a syllabus, which the teacher/coach can work to in the preparation of the sessions or lessons and the course as a whole. Perhaps readers will note my use of the word lesson here; in a teaching situation the word lesson is more appropriate than the word session, confirming a 'lesson' as a teaching activity and a 'session' as a practical coaching activity without causing confusion.

I should also remind readers that whilst, in the main, the material contained in this book is aimed at coaches for their use in coaching players, coaches can use the material as required for the coaching of coaches.

SYLLABUS

A syllabus is usually conceived initially by a potential examiner or examination body, or committee. Rarely does it indicate the relative importance of each topic within it, so it is important that the coach makes an assessment of the syllabus in some detail to check that the course preparation is satisfactory.

If an examination or a test of some kind is concerned, again the coach should check that the questions asked are completely relevant to the syllabus concerned.

DEMONSTRATION

A major requirement of any coach is to ensure that players are given the opportunity of seeing not only complete performances of any cricket skill but also part performances, highlighting the smallest details within the total skill. The highest quality of demonstration is essential and, whenever possible, it is the responsibility of the coach concerned to give the demonstration himself. It is important for coaches to practise their demonstrations to maintain standards, as players are more receptive to a demonstration from their own coach, rather than someone else. However, it is asking a lot for one coach to be the complete expert in each one of cricket's many skills and it is

Fig 69   The demonstration – it has to be good and brief.

Fig 70   The talk also has to be brief to be effective.

sometimes prudent to ask a coach with the special skills required, to do the job. Even the better player in the group can 'fill the bill' if necessary and, of course, there is the value of good visual aids, particularly the specific films.

THE VOICE

The voice and its use are of great importance to a coach, whatever his role in the cricket scene. Vary the pitch of your voice. A high pitch can more easily be heard, but a low pitch is generally more pleasant to hear. Emphasise key words, this will help your rhythm. Above all, realise its practical importance. One is not looking for anything unusual, just pleasant! Oral instructions should be considered in just the same way as a written presentation, they should be well planned and if possible supported by written notes.

NOTE-TAKING

Again this is vital to the best coaches. How, otherwise, can you fully record all the essential information on a player or a team? An old Chinese proverb says: 'The faintest ink is better than the most retentive memory'. I for one know that to be true. Once pen is put to paper you will need to think that much more and will thus clarify your own thoughts. If you write down your notes with some sort of structure, you will create less problems for yourself.

Fig 71 Richard Hadlee (New Zealand)

8 Team Management

Until I spent some time researching this subject I had the impression that any decent coach would make a capable team manager. After all, the qualities one would expect in both are not dissimilar. I still have that impression but less so, as, whilst the qualities required are similar the criteria for the two jobs vary with the brief given to each at various levels of the game. I note, for example, that the trend in junior club teams is for the manager and coach to be one and the same person. In junior schools this is not always the case. At youth representative level there is no definite pattern, but I have noticed that as the standard of play increases the managers and coaches tend to be separate. This carries through to county cricket although with some liaison between management and coach.

At Test level, however, the pattern changes completely. Team managers are only engaged for tours abroad and *coaches* are not used at all, at home or abroad. Test match teams, after all, only meet to play matches, with little or no time for sophisticated coaching; interesting, even surprising, but true. Is it a fact that once a player reaches Test match level he can no longer be concerned with coaching? It seems that way unless the team happens to be on tour, when the assistant team manager is expected to be a coach of sorts. The subjects of team management, coaching and even team selection seem to be worth exploring. There may be a formula that will allow coaching to be more effective in the game. With tongue in cheek I pose the question: in the history of Test cricket has a practising coach *ever* been a member of a Test selection committee? In this chapter I shall explore the function of team management and its relationship to coaching.

TEAM SELECTION

In the first instance I should like to think the team manager at any level is very closely concerned with team selection. He should be the 'liaison officer' of the selection committee at least, using the knowledge of and the information supplied by the coaches within the selection area concerned. There should be a system of nominating and feeding information on possible players to a *qualified* selection committee. That is, selectors who can dissect the information received properly. This does not mean that all selectors need to be technical experts on cricket. Each selector must be a part of the selection process for a specific and valid reason – as there are other reasons for selecting or not selecting a player than pure playing ability. Bearing in mind the overall responsibilities of the selection committee at all levels of the game and the effect of their decisions on each game played, it seems to me that the *selection of selectors* should be a *very* important consideration. Is it given the consideration that is warranted?

TEAM PREPARATION

Once the team is selected, the team manager must look to preparing the team or squad to perform to its maximum when required. Again, reference to expertise other than cricket may need to be considered. In this preparation section of the team manager's role the coach can again be of prime importance. Let us look at the subjects and factors to be considered.

* Consider the team's true objectives and set realistic targets that can achieve those objectives.
* Design plans (detailed if necessary) that can make the targets achievable.
* Work out a game plan (or tour plan if necessary).
* Look at the ironing out of current technical faults in players, using skill analysis techniques.
* Set individual fitness programmes (including diet) in good time – and ensure that each is properly monitored.
* Psychological preparation should be seriously considered.
* Analyse the opposition in as much detail as possible.
* Decide who does what, when and how – collectively and individually.
* When applicable, make checklists for and in co-operation with the: assistant manager; coach; captain; vice captain; groundsman; umpires; scorers; press; sponsors; medical attendants; secretariats at base and where necessary elsewhere.

If necessary delegate responsibility for: transport/travel; accommodation; team practice; cricket and other equipment; particular match information; medical supplies and first-aid; ambassadorial duties; special requirements for individual players; food and drink; photography and filming; special stationery; press liaison; finance.

Check that duplicate copies are available of all addresses, telephone numbers, telex numbers, and so on, and duplicate important keys.

From the outset, decide with the captain and coach (if available) exactly who is responsible for what – and let them know it for certain. If in doubt, consult the selection committee.

So the stage is set – the team is selected and all is prepared.

THE MATCH

I have always felt that the match starts from the time the team assembles. If possible, *all* the team should be together in the dressing-room well before the match warm-up and practice session.

From this point on, the team manager needs to be 'all things to all men'. He will realise that the captain first and the coach second will be the closest to the players and, whilst the team manager's presence is important for a good percentage of the time, it needs to be 'low profile'. If there is a low point in the team manager's activity (involving direct contact with the team) it is during the match itself, although if there is no coach all aspects of the game as it is played should be carefully studied by the team manager, who should record important points.

The Recapitulation

When the match has finished, whether it was won or lost, the team manager will be busy; congratulating and consoling. Putting everything into perspective will be the main task. Later comes the recapitulation, when all aspects of the team's and individual's performance will need to be considered in private. Progressively the team manager will discuss the match with the captain and coach and generally together they will balance the results against the original plans. At this stage it can be useful for the team manager to make his own private report either on tape or in writing.

In discussion with the captain, and selection committee if necessary, recommendations for the next match can be made. Whilst the captain will be in constant touch with the players, at some stage

an encouraging talk and maybe a question and answer session may be useful between the team manager and the players.

Feedback

Even in one match, much new cricketing information can emanate from each player. Some of it will be very obvious, but much is often less obvious; even hidden technical features of a player's performance, good and bad, will need to be spotted by the experienced coach/manager. The more difficult the problem, if there is one, the better the coach will need to be – and the more valuable he will be to both player and team. In many sports it is

Fig 72

this feature of the coach's work that brings the cheque books out and astronomical figures are bandied about. At the highest levels, with ridiculous amounts of money resting on the performance of 'star' players, one can see the logic – up to a point. Cricket coaches have no such problems, but nevertheless I find in general they have the desire to work more effectively in this area – perhaps with good reason! However, once again it is no good just seeing a performance, its significant features must be truly recorded for effective *feedback* to take place. Figures tell a story but not always a true one, and the more true information there is available to those that need it, so much the better.

SUMMARY

The formula for good team management in the simplest terms is therefore:

Prepare to select – Select – Prepare – Play – Recap – Feedback – Prepare to select again.

TIPS FOR TEAM MANAGERS

1. Do your homework on all your players – and if possible on the opposition too.
2. As in coaching, most players thrive on encouragement – but let praise be worthy praise, well earned, for effort first and results second.
3. *You* are responsible for the team's behaviour and appearance on and off the field. *You* will be the person held responsible and rightly so. Make sure *your* standards are high.
4. Look after the 'stars' last. Take a lot of trouble to ensure that the younger and maybe introverted players are given every opportunity to express themselves.
5. Remember – anybody can manage a winning team.
6. Try to create the feeling that in a cricket match teams are playing together rather than against each other. This should not dilute the will to win. Do not be remote, pop in the opposition dressing-room once in a while to make some encouraging or sociable remark. Cricket is all about respect between teams and players – or should be.
7. Do not put up with 'moaners', 'big-heads' and bullies. They do the team no good. Put them in their place firmly and politely.
8. Make your reserve players feel a part of the team. As much as possible keep them on form and fit.
9. Make time for a word with the back-room boys and girls – the umpires, the scorers, the ladies who prepare the food, in fact all those you can think of who may go unrecognised for the part they play in the game.
10. Following your visit to a club, a short hand-written note of thanks is always appreciated – especially when you go again.
11. If you and the rest of your management team (captain, coach and so on) have decided on a plan of campaign – give it a decent chance. Do not change it at the first sign of rough weather. 'When the going gets tough the tough get going!'
12. Be sure to keep your players in the picture – all the time.
13. Make a point of checking the little things; for example, is the first-aid kit aboard?

Overseas Team Management

Consult the experts in: travel; transport; medical care; insurance; diet; playing conditions; ground facilities; accommodation; finance; practice and training facilities; mail (both ways); passports; baggage; language problems; umpiring; telephone; currency; entertainment; climate. These are not in any particular order, but are all important. Link the information obtained to your detailed tour itinerary.

Fig 73   Malcolm Marshall (West Indies)

9 Cricket Games and Practices

Cricket is a most unique game: in its traditions, its homes, its personalities, its widely differing skills; even its laws, resulting in the spasmodic and sometimes minimal physical involvement of its players. These facets of the game sometimes tend to repel rather than attract even those who may wish to know something of it. The solid preservation of its values gives the character of cricket a mellow arrogance that can irk those who are not involved. Yet this, together with its almost peculiar design of play, is somehow part of its charm. In a way, one grows up into cricket, if properly exposed to it. But this 'proper exposure' can be interpreted in different ways. The game does not give up its rewards easily to those who have little natural ability. For example, the rules are such that in any match, particularly for a batsman, one mistake or misfortune can be something of a disaster at the worst, or an extreme disappointment at best.

If the game is to be properly learned, there must be within it the opportunity for lots of activity and full participation for young players in their early years. This is what 'properly exposed' really means. In many other sports, both individual and team, some of which are new to this country, full participation has been the theme projected with some success. This applies very much in the field of physical education. In the not too distant past cricket, particularly in schools, was being ignored by those young people, mainly boys, who once would have been considered the players of the future. Understandably so! Who wants to learn a game by watching most of the time? Nobody, I'll be bound! Thank goodness, today the situation has changed considerably. A host of cricket games and practices give full participation to all in the learning period. Batsmen who are bowled out first ball receive lesser penalties than being banished to the pavilion, bowlers *have* to bowl, fielders in teams of eight and six are required to exhaust themselves, rather than the opposite.

These attitudes within the 'new' cricket games for young players have their critics as one would expect – but progressively less so, as the great majority of players and coaches recognise the outstanding benefits that come from creating interest and participation for all, rather than the highly talented few.

Having said this, I very definitely make the point that the traditional (normal) eleven-a-side game should *not be excluded* altogether from the training of any young cricketer from the age of ten upwards. Depending upon the ability and number of those available it should be gradually introduced, if only to expose them to the 'slings and arrows'. In general, the better the players and teams, the more they should play the traditional eleven-a-side game. However, a good coach should be on hand to ensure that all the players get a fair chance to participate in the game. As I have already suggested,

93

there are few guarantees for the players in the traditional eleven-a-side match. As a batsman your day can be cut very short on the bounce of the ball. As a fielder chance again dictates the level of your participation and not a very even chance at that. Only one bowler can bowl at any one time and only two all the time if the game demands. Yet this wheel of fortune, this lack of guaranteed participation, in some obtuse way plays its part in cricket's attraction. It stimulates a situation as only the knife-edge of a *once only* chance can, and in doing so it also creates opportunities, even an addiction to live with the ideals of the true sportsman.

This is why we need to condition our young players for achievement, by giving them the chance they otherwise may never have of developing their skills outside the type of game we all know awaits them.

The following itemises some of the requirements from cricket games and practices if they are to be effective. They must always be fun, create interest, include incentives and rewards. They must also:

* Be designed to give as strong a link as possible with the real game of cricket.
* Introduce experience in the pressures that may be encountered in cricket, i.e. making a run-out with a split second decision, taking a vital high catch, taking a wicket or scoring winning runs in the last over of a match.
* Include a strong element of controlled physical training.
* Recognise that the improved performance of a skill can be achieved by a high number of repetitions of the correct movements in that skill. Games and practices should follow this principle when possible.
* Aim at maximum participation of individuals without detracting from the main object of the exercise.
* Set higher targets as experience grows. This will extend the skills of the players concerned.
* Recognise that the recording and acknowledgement of a performance gives a player a sense of achievement. If a player knows he has improved, he is likely to improve more – and quicker.

A few suitable games and practices are described here. Coaches will discover and maybe design many more to add to their repertoires. Remember to use them only if they follow the principles noted above.

TEAM CRICKET

Team cricket can be played equally effectively with a soft or a hard ball – depending upon environment, equipment available, and so on.

1. Each team shall comprise eight players.
2. The length of the pitch shall be 18 yards (16 yards for under eleven cricket). As normal for hard balls.
3. Junior indoor cricket stumps should be used, when possible. If not available, any suitable alternative may be used at the discretion of the organiser.
4. Each game shall consist of one innings per team, each innings to be of twelve (six ball) overs duration (sixteen or twenty overs when time permits).
5. The batting side shall be divided into pairs, each pair batting for three overs

Fig 74   Edgbaston in July: the scene of the U11 Softball (Team
Cricket) finals. Four games are taking place at the same
time on this famous ground. A pointer for club coaching
days. Note the video cameraman making a record of the
game. A marvellous coaching feature.

(four or five overs in sixteen or twenty
overs games).

6. No player on the fielding side may
bowl more than a quarter of the total
overs (i.e. four in a sixteen over game).
The wicket-keeper may not bowl.

7. Each team shall commence batting
with a team score of 200 runs.

8. Each time a wicket falls, runs must be
deducted from the team score (six for
under eleven, eight for under thirteen, ten
for under fifteen and so on).

9. When a batsman is dismissed, he
should immediately change ends with the
non-striker (on all but the last ball of the
over or after a run-out).

10. It is recommended that no fielder
shall be allowed to field within eleven
yards of the batsman's middle stump,
except behind the wicket on the off-side
(eight yards when playing with a soft
ball). (Call *no ball* for contraventions of
this rule.)

11. The Laws of Cricket shall apply
outside specific local rules defined by the
organiser.

Note   Cricket Umpiring and Scoring by
Tom Smith is a particularly useful book
for coaches.

Important Features

Team cricket has a number of interesting
features.

95

1. It rewards the team playing the most enterprising cricket.

2. It can easily be controlled by one person, if necessary. This is a significant advantage if played at school, when only one teacher may be available to supervise.

3. It involves all the players in all of cricket's major skills (batting, bowling, fielding and wicket-keeping).

4. A complete game, with a definite result, can be played within the hour (one hour thirty minutes if playing sixteen overs per side).

5. The problems of keeping individual scores and bowling analyses are removed – again a significant benefit, when only one adult is available for supervision and organisation.

Variations of team cricket to suit the needs of the particular situation are obviously possible and desirable and these variations can be developed by enterprising organisers. For example, when team cricket is played indoors with a soft ball, six-a-side scoring can be used.

SIX-A-SIDE CRICKET

This is another excellent and nationally popular game played mainly indoors.

Equipment

The 'Reader Indoor Cricket Ball', obtainable from leading sports retailers, has been specially developed for this mainly indoor game and is strongly recommended, although tennis balls or similar may be used. Normal cricket balls can be used when playing outside. Portable stumps or suitable replicas are necessary and a good playing surface is essential. Various

forms of artificial surfaces can be laid if necessary and available.

When hard cricket balls are used all normal protective equipment should be used. Tennis balls may be used for indoor school matches, in which case minimum equipment is sufficient and there is no need for special surfaces.

Facilities

Sports halls or gymnasiums measuring a minimum of $100 \times 60 \times 20$ feet are recommended for adult games although this can be varied to suit local conditions. When played by youngsters with tennis balls the area can be appropriately less.

Playing Regulations

The Laws of Cricket shall apply with the exception of the following playing regulations:

1. Teams shall consist of six players each.

2. Each match shall consist of one innings per team.

3. Each innings shall consist of a maximum of twelve six ball overs.

4. No bowler shall bowl more than three overs. In the event of a bowler becoming incapacitated, the over shall be completed by a bowler who has not bowled three overs even if he bowled the preceding over.

5. There shall be a ten minute interval between innings.

6. Two batsmen shall be at the wicket at all times during an innings. In the event of a team losing five wickets within the permitted twelve overs, the last man shall continue batting with the fifth man out remaining at the wicket as a runner.

Fig 75   Indoor six-a-side cricket – now a game for all ages.

7. When a batsman reaches a personal total of twenty-five he shall retire but may return to the crease in the event of his side being dismissed within the twelve overs. Retired batsmen must return in the order of their retirement and take the place of the retiring or dismissed batsman. Two 'live' batsmen shall be at the wicket until such time as the fifth wicket has fallen.

8. If, in the opinion of the umpire, negative or short-pitched bowling becomes persistent he shall call and signal no ball.

9. The laws relating to wides shall be strictly interpreted by the umpire.

Results

The team scoring the most runs in its innings shall be the winner. If the scores of both teams are equal, then the team losing the fewer wickets shall be the winner. If the teams are still equal, then each member of both teams shall bowl one ball (overarm): the team hitting the stumps the greater number of times shall be the winner.

Scoring

The scoring for six-a-side cricket indoors shall take place as follows:

1. A ball struck to hit the boundary wall behind the bowler without touching the floor or any other wall or ceiling shall count six runs. If, however, the ball touches the floor but does not touch any of the other walls or the ceiling and hits the boundary wall, then it shall count as four runs.
2. A ball struck to hit the ceiling or one or more of the side or back walls shall count one run, even if the ball subsequently hits the boundary wall. Two additional runs shall be scored if the batsmen complete a run. (If the ball is struck to hit the ceiling or side or back wall and a batsman is then run out one run shall be scored.)
3. Two runs shall be scored if the striker plays the ball and it does not hit a wall direct and the batsmen complete a run.
4. A bye shall count as one run if the ball hits a wall; a leg-bye shall count as one run if the ball hits a wall. In each case if the batsmen complete a run, two additional runs shall be scored.
5. Two byes or two leg-byes shall be scored if the batsmen complete a run without the ball hitting a wall.
6. No ball:
    (a) If the batsmen do not run when a no ball is called, a penalty of one run shall be credited under extras. This shall apply even though the ball hits the ceiling, a side or a back wall.
    (b) If the batsman does not strike the ball and completes a run, two runs shall be credited under extras. This shall apply whether or not the ball hits the ceiling, a side or a back wall.
    (c) If a striker hits a no ball the number of runs resulting, as specified in Rules 1, 2 and 3 above, shall be added to his score but not the penalty in addition.
7. Wide:
    (a) If a wide ball is called, a penalty of one run shall be credited under extras even though the ball hits the ceiling, a side or a back wall.
    (b) Two runs shall be credited under extras for every run completed by the batsmen but not the penalty in addition. This shall apply whether or not the ball hits the ceiling, a side or a back wall.
8. An overthrow hitting any wall shall count as one run to the batsman. (The batsmen shall not change ends.)
9. No runs shall be scored if a batsman is caught out off the walls or ceiling.

Methods of Dismissal

Apart from the normal methods of dismissal contained in the Laws of Cricket, the following variations shall apply:

1. The batsman shall be caught out by a fieldsman after the ball has hit the ceiling, the netting or any wall except directly from the boundary wall, provided the ball has not touched the floor.
2. The last not-out batsman shall be given out if the non-striker running with him is run out.
3. The batsman or the non-striker shall be given not out if the ball rebounds from a wall or ceiling and hits a wicket without being touched by a fieldsman.

Note. All players should wear the normal

accepted cricket clothing and equipment. This includes wicket-keepers wearing pads.

TRIOS TOURNAMENT

Over many years trios tournaments (three-a-side) have been popular in the north. They make excellent contributions to club gala days and indeed are a lot of fun when played as a knock-out competition.

Any number between eight and sixteen teams can provide a good day's cricket, regulating the overs per team in each game accordingly.

Sample Rules

1. Each innings will consist of an agreed number of six ball overs, unless all three members of the batting 'trio' are dismissed before the total number of overs due have been bowled (organiser to decide number of overs and so on).
2. The third batsman, if necessary, will continue his innings alone until all overs due are completed or he is dismissed.
3. When the third batsman is continuing his innings alone he can only be run out at the bowler's end when he has passed a line marked on the centre of the pitch. Having passed this line he cannot return to his crease. If he has not reached the centre line when attempting a run he can be run out at the wicket-keeper's end.
4. One member of the trio will keep wicket, the other two members will bowl alternately from opposite ends.
5. When fielding, three members of another trio will make the number of fielders up to six. (A rota system amongst the non-playing teams should apply.)
6. The winner of each game will be the

trio scoring the greater number of runs, irrespective of the number of wickets fallen. In the event of a tie it is usual for each team to let one batsman bat for one over.
7. All the normal rules of cricket apply except in so far as they are amended by the tournament organiser.

3–2–1 CRICKET

For a change this can add a new dimension to a normal cricket practice game between two teams.

Rules

1. Each batsman is allowed three 'good' balls.
2. If the batsman scores off the first ball he gets a bonus of two runs. If he scores off the second ball the bonus is one. If he scores off the third ball there is no bonus. If he fails to score off three 'good' balls the batsman is out.
3. If the batsman's partner is run out in trying to run a bye, the batsman (on strike) is out.
4. The umpire shall call *ball one, ball two, ball three* for each 'good' ball delivered. If a ball is adjudged to be not good (i.e. not in reasonable reach for the batsman to make a scoring stroke) a *wide* (one run) shall be awarded.

CONTINUOUS CRICKET

I have included notes on this game as it is ideal to finish off an indoor coaching session. It provides lots of fun over a short period of up to half an hour.

There are two teams. The ball is

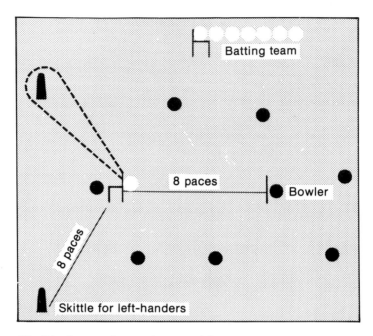

Fig 76   Layout for continuous cricket.

bowled to the No. 1 batsman. If he hits the ball, he drops the bat, runs around the post as indicated in Fig 76 to score a run, picks up his bat and prepares to face the bowler again. The ball is fielded and thrown to the bowler who immediately bowls again, whether the batsman has returned or not. A run is scored each time the batsman runs around the post and back to his wicket without being out. The batsman is out if the bowler hits the wicket, if he hits his own wicket, and if he is caught from a hit.

When the No. 1 batsman is out, he immediately drops the bat and No. 2 batsman runs to pick it up and take his place. The bowler may continue to bowl during the change-over and if he hits the wicket, No. 2 is out. Then No. 3 batsman runs in, and so on until the whole team is out. The teams then change over. The side scoring the greater number of runs wins.

MINI-CRICKET

One of the many success stories in the development of cricket in recent years has been the recognition, albeit limited at the time of writing, of the full-time Youth Cricket Development Officer. Nottinghamshire and Lancashire County Cricket Clubs are leading the way in linking the requirements of professional and recreational cricket to give maximum opportunity to young players in their counties. The post has great potential.

John Cope, the man concerned with Nottinghamshire cricket, has developed a simple cricket game from those described earlier in this chapter. He has called it

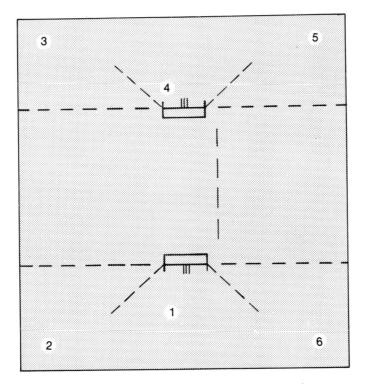

Fig 77   The playing area for mini-cricket, showing the positions of the fielding discs.

mini-cricket, and in my opinion it is a cricket game that has much potential in primary and junior schools. Hence my reason for describing it in some detail here. I thank John for giving me permission to reproduce the following.

Mini-cricket can be played indoors or outdoors and requires the minimum of equipment. All you need is light bats or bat shapes; light plastic ball or tennis ball; two sets of stumps or skittles; six fielders' marking discs; and a scoresheet or blackboard.

Mini-cricket is ideal for eight to twelve year olds, but is fun for all. There are six players in a team and everyone bats and bowls in turn. One game lasts approximately forty minutes.

How to Play

Team captains toss a coin to decide which team will bat first. The batting team then organise themselves into three pairs, while each member of the fielding team takes up position on one of the six fielding discs (Fig 77). The fielder on disc one will be the first bowler. The fielder on disc four will be the first wicket-keeper. These two fielders may move their discs to convenient positions. Outfielders must be in contact with their disc (positioned approximately forty-five degrees behind the stumps) until the bowler starts to run up to bowl.

The batting team starts with 100 runs. The first pair of the batting team bat for

101

two overs (six balls per over) whether they are out or not. The batsmen *must run* every time the ball is hit. They must also run for byes and leg-byes. Every time a wicket falls, the batsmen change ends – except after a run out.

The bowling must be overarm and take place from the same end throughout the game. Six legitimate balls must be bowled by each bowler. No balls and wides count as one run and another ball must be bowled.

At the end of every over, the fielding team moves round one place in a clockwise direction and the batsmen change ends.

At the end of each innings (six overs) each member of the fielding team will have taken up each position and each member of the batting team will have batted.

At the end of the first two overs, the first pair of batsmen retire and are replaced by the second pair. After two more overs they are replaced by the third pair. When the first team have all batted, the second team bat for their full six overs. When both teams have batted for six overs, the team with the highest score wins the match.

When a batsman is out, three runs are deducted from the batting team's score. A batsman can be out by being run out, caught, stumped or bowled, hitting his wicket or leg before wicket.

Advice to Players

Batsmen: be ready to steal runs. Call to your partner. Reach for the crease.

Fielders: be ready for catches and run outs. Watch the ball. Move quickly to the ball. Throw quickly and accurately.

At the end of the game, thank the umpire and shake hands with your opponents. Help to collect the equipment.

Hints to Organisers

BOUNDARIES

If the game is played indoors, give four runs for a direct hit onto the wall behind the bowler. Allow the ball to remain in play off all the other walls.

When played out of doors, impose boundaries with discretion but allow continuous play whenever possible. If boundaries are too simple, it spoils the continuity of the game.

FIELD PLACINGS

Follow the recommendations in Fig 77. Ensure that the fielder on disc five (disc three if the batsman is a left-hander) is not in danger from a hit to leg by the batsman.

UMPIRING

It is not difficult to act as umpire and scorer at the same time. It is also possible to use children as umpires, this will allow more than one game to be played at a time.

When there is the likelihood of a run out, the umpire is advised to move quickly to a position between discs five and six. This will give a good view of both ends.

PRACTICES

Slip Catching

This practice is as near as possible to the real thing. It is suitable for a wicket-

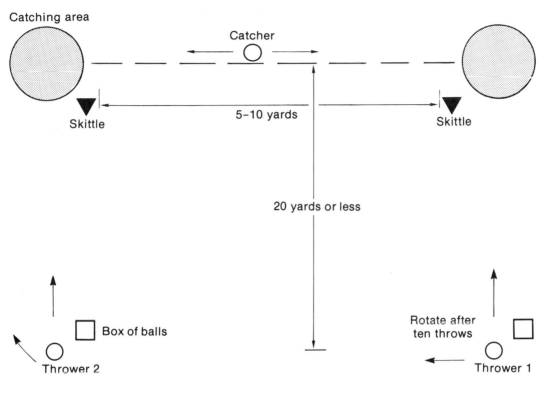

Fig 78 Pressure catching.

keeper and up to six other players.

The thrower aims a cricket ball at shoulder height slightly to the off-side of a batsman who cuts the ball at various angles to slips, gulley and wicket-keeper. After about fifteen to twenty throws, with the exception of the wicket-keeper, the rest rotate to give everyone the slip catching practice. The same type of practice can be undertaken on the leg-side, feeding catches to the short leg positions and the wicket-keeper.

In warm conditions, close catchers need lots of this sort of practice. The coach should ensure also that it progressively extends the catchers throughout the session, both in the pace of the ball and in the stretching and one-handed catching of the fielder.

Pressure Catching (Fig 78)

A single group of three can gain much from this activity, or a number of teams of three can compete. Two throwers feed a fielder sprinting between fixed points to make each catch – or stop. A distance of five yards may be set, but this can be varied as required by the coach.

Each player in a team should make twelve catches or stops before moving in a clockwise direction to all the other players in the same practice. If it is a team competition, the winners are those who reach their original positions first.

Pressure Fielding (Fig 79)

Again, this is a realistic team practice. The thrower either rolls or throws the ball to one of the outfielders in the square, calling him by name as he does so. As soon as the ball is released, the batsman starts running. The fielder returns the ball to the wicket-keeper in an effort to run out one of the batsmen. The group periodically rotate.

This principle can apply to any of the outfielding or, for that matter, infielding positions. The coach should, as always, aim for maximum quality participation. The thrower will perhaps be more effective using a bat to direct the ball either on the ground or in the air to the fielders concerned.

Throwing at a Football (Fig 80)

1. Divide the class into two teams.
2. Each team throws a tennis ball to hit the football and knock it over their opponents' front line.
3. No one is to throw the ball from in front of their own front line.
4. Start by using one tennis ball at each end and gradually introduce more balls.

Bowling at Targets (Fig 81)

Player A has ten balls and sees how many he can score. Player B acts as wicket-keeper and calls out the number of points scored. Player B then has ten balls.

Players A and B can either compete against each other or add their scores

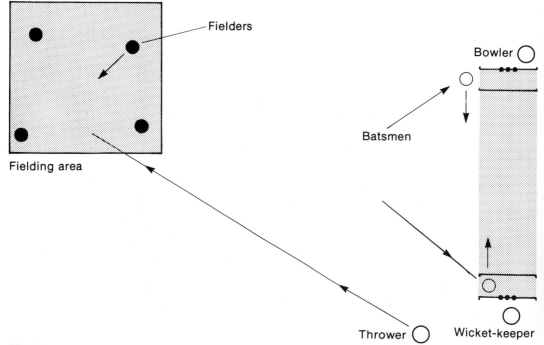

Fig 79 Pressure fielding.

together and compete against other couples in the group.

PROFICIENCY AWARD CRICKET

Whilst NCA have designed the Proficiency Award Scheme mainly to encourage young players between nine and sixteen years of age, the tests themselves and the practices leading up to them are marvellous as competitive games for all ages. There are lots of batting practices, shuttle runs, target throwing, tests of strength, accuracy and so on, most of which can provide the interest, activity and variety so necessary in the repertoire of the good coach. One can even use the

results as the basis of a competition between coaches.

ARRANGING LEAGUES AND TOURNAMENTS

Many is the time when coaches are required to set up some form of cricket competition involving numbers of teams or groups. What a nuisance it can be if you are not quite familiar with the procedures necessary to make a decent job of it. You will certainly be respected by all concerned if you take the trouble to present results properly and in a manner that can be understood by all. Even though the following notes may appear to be very simple I am sure you will

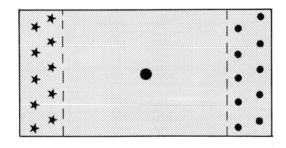

Fig 80 Throwing at a football.

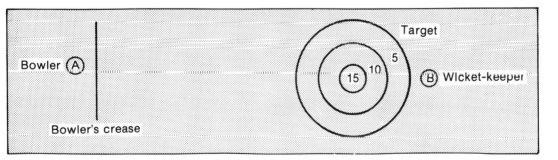

Fig 81 Bowling at targets.

nevertheless find them useful.

In most schools and clubs it is often necessary to arrange both leagues and knock-out tournaments for major and minor games. Here are some simple methods and formulae for arranging such competitions.

Arranging Leagues

In a league where each team plays every other team once, the number of games which will need to be arranged is determined by the following formula:

$$\frac{\text{no. of teams involved} \times (\text{no. of teams} - 1)}{2}$$

Thus in an eight-team league the number of games will be: $8 \times (8 - 1) \div 2 = 28$ games.

If, however, the teams play each other both at home and away the number of games will be doubled and the formula for an eight-team league will be simply: $8 \times (8 - 1) = 56$ games.

Arranging the Fixtures

Once you know the number of teams and games involved in completing a league competition the arranging of fixtures can be done by the following simple method.

Let us assume that six teams only are involved. First, write down the number of teams as below:

6 v (1)
5 v 2
4 v 3

Leaving team (1) fixed in its starting position revolve the other teams anti-clockwise around it, thus:

2 v (1)	3 v (1)	4 v (1)	5 v (1)
6 v 3	2 v 4	3 v 5	4 v 6
5 v 4	6 v 5	2 v 6	3 v 2

If home and away matches are played the fixtures will merely be repeated.

If there is an odd number of teams in the league, say seven, arrange the first matches as shown below:

0 v (1)
7 v 2
6 v 3
5 v 4

Then proceed exactly as before, but wherever the zero appears there will be no game; thus the second and third series of games will be:

2 v (1)	3 v (1)
0 v 3 (no game)	2 v 4
7 v 4	0 v 5 (no game)
6 v 5	7 v 6

Arranging Knock-out Competitions

In any knock-out competition, the number of games to be played is always one less than the number of teams (or individuals) entered. If the number of teams entered is a power of 2 (i.e. 4, 8, 16, 32, and so on) then the procedure is simple (Fig 82). If the number of teams entered is not a power of 2, it must be made so by means of 'byes'.

Thus, for example, if 12 teams have entered, 4 byes will be required (12 + 4 = 16). In addition, if the number of byes is odd, the extra bye is placed at one end of the draw sheet as shown in Fig 83.

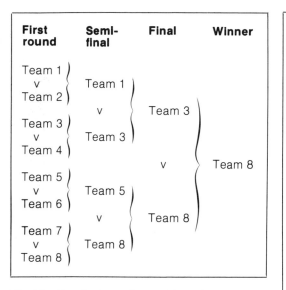

First round	Semi-final	Final	Winner
Team 1			
v	Team 1		
Team 2			
	v	Team 3	
Team 3			
v	Team 3		
Team 4			
		v	Team 8
Team 5			
v	Team 5		
Team 6			
	v	Team 8	
Team 7			
v	Team 8		
Team 8			

Fig 82   Simple draw sheet with no byes.

First round	Second round	Semi-final	Final	Winner
1 (bye)	1			
	v	2		
2 (bye)	2			
		v	6	
3				
v	4			
4		6		
	v			
5				
v	6			
6			v	13
7				
v	8			
8				
	v	9		
9				
v	9			
10		v	13	
11				
v	11	13		
12				
	v			
13 (bye)	13			

Fig 83   Thirteen teams entered, byes.

Fig 84   John Emburey (England)

10 Cricket and Education

COMMENT

More often than not these days, the most evident theme on the front page of any newspaper will be *tragedy*. In fact many readers will turn to the sports pages to give their day a better start. Dare we think that by linking sport with education more closely we could have an influence for the better on life in general? I doubt whether we could make it worse. After all, cliché though it may be, sport *is* a religion of the twentieth century; at least, it appears to be in nearly every home and work-place in the country. Like life sport is competitive and like life sport is full of the 'slings and arrows'. Unlike life, however, it allows its participants to experience those 'slings and arrows' without harm. The question is, how do we go about it?

Firstly, and most importantly, we should let education and sport come together in harmony with the certainty that they have much to offer each other. The highest standards need to be set to identify the sports that meet the *true* needs of education in terms of exposure to 'life'. Sports not containing the elements required should not be included in any training college syllabus or school curriculum. Neither, within the new programmes, should excellence be considered before involvement and skill training for all. Excellence can be encouraged as just one part of involvement, but not fanatically. We have seen what fanaticism in sport produces!

I am a cricketer, and well aware of what my sport does for the young people who get the opportunity to know it early in life. The following examples may speak for cricket and many other sports too.

* Children who are exposed to and sympathetically taught to play cricket at school come away with many advantages. They need not have the physical make-up of an athlete, as there are enough roles in the game for all shapes and sizes, young or old for that matter. Obviously physical fitness plays its part as competition becomes greater, but other assets are equally, if not more, important. Cricket and citizenship are synonymous.
* Nowadays cricket is a game of participation for all, as its variations become increasingly popular. National club competitions range from 'under eleven' to 'over fifty'.
* The investment in teaching cricket at school is spread over a lifetime of interest and participation. Perhaps the game's greatest asset is in its thousands of homes (up to ten thousand clubs) for boys and girls from all walks of life, offering a wide variety of social contact that can only contribute to a happy family life.
* Cricket is a great leveller, as its best exponents can fail just as easily as its less gifted players can quickly improve and succeed.
* Cricket has long traditions and a magic folklore. Ethics and compassion

are lessons in the game. The term 'it's not cricket' did not come about by accident.

* Cricket is local, regional, national and international. It involves millions of people and its influence is such that it touches everyday working life without harm. In fact, those that play, or have played, or wanted to play, share a companionship tinged with a sense of humour that conveys more than anything else my reasons for promoting the game with our young people.

* Cricket through its long traditions has created a bond between races that can be seen and appreciated from Test match arena to the junior school games lesson.

* Cricket is complex enough for the academic and simple enough for the practical man. Perhaps therein lies its fascination.

Is it not possible, therefore, that there might be a role for sport and cricket in particular in the development of education – or vice versa, especially if both are prepared to change? Could we both not look again and recognise that it *may*, if we can honestly co-operate, be cheap at the price?

The following perhaps profound but in my opinion realistic proposals might be worth trying – if not, why not?

1. Let those in sports education consider working more realistic hours inside and outside the school curriculum – on Saturdays and in traditional school holidays and so on. (Maybe they do already, but is it official?)

2. Let those in education acquire a greater appreciation of the more complex sports and therefore become far more qualified to teach the skills. At the moment, comparatively little time is given to them in college programmes. In the majority of colleges of higher education, no more than fifty hours of cricket instruction is given in three years, and in many cases much less.

3. Put the acquisition of skill at least alongside the need for physical fitness (one will then go more naturally with the other).

4. Recognise that the strong promotion of good sportsmanship and fair play is a major contribution to education.

5. Look for stronger links between schools and clubs, giving a more realistic use of available facilities and equipment. This would open the door to an easier placement of school children and those leaving school, into sound and well-established organisations.

6. Look to more visits from sporting personalities who can project the dignity of sport.

7. Engage expert coaches, both professional and amateur, paid and voluntary, to work with the schools' teachers of sport in the school programme of sport.

8. Use television and video to promote what is good in sport and to really decry what is bad – and we have all seen what is bad!

CRICKET COACHING IN CLUBS AND SCHOOLS

Cricket in clubs and in many junior and primary schools has never been healthier, as the game, now in many forms, has maintained its popularity. Some may say that it is entirely due to the sophisticated television coverage of Test matches, but this must be an unrealistic comment. The real reason is without doubt the tremendous work of an army of coaches and club officials of varying commitment. The dream of one coach in every cricket club is not so far away as one would imagine.

Club Coaching

The success of coaching in clubs is very much related to the development of the clubs themselves – and for this the National Cricket Association should take great credit.

In recent years help, necessarily financial, has come from various sources mentioned elsewhere in this book, but as always the really hard work falls on the shoulders of the usual hard core of enthusiasts. The effect of the family, one of a cricket club's greatest assets, has also played its part. At one end of the scale, the adult player with a family has no longer been content to see the demise of his game in state schools and the consequent lack of opportunity for his sons. He has instigated in the very active cricket clubs of today the need to develop the club as a centre of social activity, where the whole family can enjoy a pleasant atmosphere, not so readily available elsewhere outside the home. Players' wives (a considerable number) must also have influenced the change as they want to participate, with their family, in the social life of the cricket club. The growth of junior cricket is an almost inevitable result of these attitudes, especially when encouraged by league competitions and, progressively, the possibility of travel and representative cricket from the age of eleven upwards.

At the other end of the scale, young enthusiasts encouraged to join thriving junior sections of cricket clubs have come under the influence of former players, turned coaches. These youngsters have themselves played their part in the success stories, very often bringing their parents to the club to support them in the widest sense. It may not be generally known, but there are upwards of ten thousand cricket clubs in the United Kingdom and this is a very stable number.

ORGANISATION
OF CLUB COACHING

With the prevalent attitudes described, it is not difficult for even one enthusiast to persuade club committees of the need for a junior section. Once this need has been recognised, the prevailing mood will almost certainly escalate into the formation of what may be generally termed a Junior and Youth Committee. On this committee, however small, there should be at least a couple of former players with an enthusiasm to develop the decision. Action does and will need to be taken under various headings:

1. Establish a leader for the young players.
2. Try to ensure that the leader and hopefully one or two helpers attend a basic NCA coaching course to obtain some ideas on how to coach juniors and organise the junior and youth section of the club.
3. Look to establishing an area for juniors to play a match practice without interference.
4. With regard to establishing such an area, investigate the possibilities of pro-

viding a non-turf pitch, but in any case ensure that juniors play and practise on the best possible surface.

5. Start your junior sections with players aged under thirteen and progress to other age groups as the section becomes stronger in every way.

6. Make sure your junior section is financially sound so that reasonable equipment and proper games can be played. Consider sponsored Proficiency Award ('Test') Cricket.

7. Give your aims and ambitions for your junior and youth sections plenty of publicity and it will pay dividends.

School Coaching

Whilst the development of cricket in schools and clubs has many features in common, there are significant differences that need to be recognised. We must differentiate between the various types of schools before we can look at their potential.

Firstly, let us consider the primary and junior schools. These schools (several thousand of them) are perhaps the biggest potential source of cricket development in the United Kingdom. As I have already stated more than once, if a youngster has not experienced cricket in some form before the age of fourteen it is unlikely that he will take up the game after that. Perhaps these days under sixteen cricket will encourage some, but these will be a minority.

The attitude of the school teacher, and for that matter the PE profession as a whole, towards encouraging the playing of cricket in schools must be considered. Hopefully they will realise the educational potential in cricket, already stated in this chapter. Hundreds of thousands of cricketers throughout the land prove weekly that cricket can be a most valuable tool for education and, as such, should be considered in the curriculum, at least of the junior schools. There is nothing like sending children home from school in a happy frame of mind to encourage them to look forward to tomorrow. Cricket can do this and educate at the same time. Teachers – why not give it a try? Learn to set up some of the games depicted in Chapter 9; I am sure you will enjoy the participation as much as the children.

Much of what I have said about cricket in primary and junior schools is probably already in being and will continue to develop. I am not so optimistic for the comprehensive secondary schools, most of which are without reasonable facilities and committed teachers/coaches. I could make a case for spending a fortune at this level, but I cannot honestly try. From the outside there seem to be so many problems and pressures on the pupils and staff, that a more radical view might be more credible, effective and acceptable.

Without reasonable facilities we all know that it is extremely difficult to play a game, let alone practise. In addition there are important examinations to prepare for and competition from an increasing number of emerging sports. One does not wish to ignore the challenge, but being realistic and accepting the need for a new point of view, I am sure a better case can be made for cricket in these secondary schools being transferred to clubs as an activity to last throughout the summer. After all, with cricket being a dry weather sport and the state secondary school season seldom lasting more than seven or eight weeks the proverbial 'brick wall' looms very near.

This is not the case in public schools as, traditionally, the game of cricket is part of their heritage and in most cases must be passed on at all costs. In fact, the masters in charge of sport in public schools have a definite policy of learning the game and its coaching for that very reason.

In general, however, the strengthening of links between schools with little chance of developing cricket and their local cricket clubs offers the greatest potential. Apart from rationalising finance, the continuity and availability of help and expertise make the thought very feasible, even desirable. The message is simply this: those with an interest in cricket who work in schools of minimum cricket activity should contact their local club and enquire as to the possible chances of some sort of co-operation. In particular, the use of the club facilities and maybe coaching expertise in and out of the holiday periods might be a real source of saving – and not only to the school. It may be that in the prevailing circumstances, local or education authorities or an individual sponsor will make a contribution towards this combining of resources. In cases where local school facilities are good and under-utilised in the summer holiday, it surely must be logical to look at a reciprocal arrangement.

Fig 85   Edgbaston – if our young cricketers learned to play the game on surfaces just a little like this, there would never be any shortage of good batsmen and bowlers at the highest level.

113

These comments on cricket in schools have as yet made little mention of the considerable amount of cricket still played in schools generally and at local, county and national representative level. Mention should be made here of the tremendous work over many years of the English Schools Cricket Association. ESCA can never be appreciated enough for what it has done – and for that matter still does – for English cricket. Its national officials know more Test match players than the Test match selection panel, so many great players have worn the ESCA cap. Anyone reading these words who knows of a school or a schoolboy that wishes to play cricket at school and does not, need only search for the County Schools Cricket Association. I have never known one of the stalwarts involved not try and help. Where there is a will there is a way, and if cricket is wanted by a school there is indeed a well-charted path to follow.

USEFUL NOTES ON JUNIOR CRICKET

Both NCA and ESCA in their responsibilities for junior cricket have laid down

Fig 86　Two Neils, Lenham (Sussex) and Lloyd (Yorkshire), opening the batting for England Schools U15 eleven 198—. Both boys scored centuries in the match and went on to represent England Young Cricketers in U19 international matches. These lads are representative of thousands of young cricketers; not so much for their ability and success, but in their attitude towards the game. These are the sort of young players who make cricket coaching so rewarding.

Age Group	Size of Ball	Size of Bat	Stumps	Length of Pitch
Under 7	4¾oz	3	27 × 8in	16 yards
Under 9	4¾oz	4	27 × 8in	17 yards
Under 10	4¾oz	4/5	27 × 8in	18 yards
Under 11	4¾oz	5/6	27 × 8in	19 yards
Under 12	4¾oz	6/H	27 × 8in	20 yards
Under 13	4¾oz	6/H	27 × 8in	21 yards
Under 14	5½oz	6/H	28 × 9in	22 yards
Under 15	5½oz	H/FS	28 × 9in	22 yards

Fig 87

guidelines for the benefit of junior cricket. The more important information is reproduced here.

Age Groups

Juniors will be considered up to the under fifteen age group and all information given refers to boys and girls.

The date and time used to indicate age groups shall be midnight on 31 August of the year previous to the cricket season under consideration. A player who is thirteen years old on 31 August of the previous year will not be eligible to play in under thirteen matches, whilst a player who becomes thirteen on 1 September of the previous year will be eligible to play under thirteen cricket the following calendar year.

Equipment Recommendations

There is a wide range both in the size and quality of bats. The size of the bat used will depend much on the height and size of the player and therefore the sizes recommended in Fig 87 only give a general picture of the requirements. Advice should be sought from leading coaches on how to select your bat, and how to clean and care for cricket gear.

Batsmen should be instructed to wear pads, batting gloves and a protector. Wicket-keepers should wear pads, gloves and a protector.

Fig 88 Abdul Qadir (Pakistan)

11 Coaching Miscellanea

LIFE SAVING

During the NCA Advanced Coaching Course, the Royal Life Saving Society are engaged and willingly give instruction in resuscitation techniques. At first, I thought this far removed from cricket, but I have since heard of two instances where coaches at opposite ends of the country have put their instruction to good use in club nets and given resuscitation in an emergency. I do not wish to dwell on or detail either incident, but what a wonderful feeling it is to know that qualified action has possibly saved two young lives.

All self-respecting cricket coaches should be able to apply basic resuscitation techniques; that is, the opening of the airway, artificial ventilation and external compression.

I strongly recommend that you write for appropriate literature to either the St John Ambulance Association or The Royal Life Saving Society. It will be well worthwhile.

FIRST AID

Whilst one does not expect coaches to be experts in all forms of first aid, it is the coach's duty to see that wherever and whenever cricket is played, a well-stocked first aid kit is available. Let me put it this way – how would you feel if, on the occasion it is desperately needed, you have let the side down?

A good first aid box should contain:

1. Pain reliever agents: spray; soluble aspirin.
2. Strapping and bandages: two 3 × 6 inch crêpe bandages; two 3 inch Elastoplast adhesive bandages; one triangular bandage; a roll of cotton wool.
3. Cleansing agents and dressings: antiseptic cream; hydrogen peroxide; gauze swabs; cotton bandages; Vaseline gauze; cotton wool swabs.
4. Miscellaneous: scissors; sterile needles (for blisters); clinical thermometer; eyebath; inflatable/Kramer splints; first aid manual; smelling salts.

INJURIES IN CRICKET

Every coach is responsible for each cricketer in his charge, but no matter what safety precautions are taken accidents will happen and you must be ready to deal with them.

Realise that:

* Dealing with sports injuries is a highly specialised business.
* You are not (necessarily) qualified to diagnose and treat injury.
* If in any doubt, you should do nothing until the qualified personnel arrive.

Always keep calm, and if necessary prevent others – no matter how well meaning – from attempting to 'make the patient comfortable'. This is not to suggest that as a coach you should ignore requests for help from injured sportsmen. You should recognise that pain is a symptom and as such should always be treated seriously. However, hasty, ill-considered action is seldom for the best.

INSURANCE

I wondered at first if the question of insurance was worth mentioning here. Then I remembered the legal enquiries I have had from parties looking to sue not the club or the school, but the *coach* for supposed negligence in the most remote of cricket net situations. Not long after one of these enquiries I read of a coach in another sport being sued for £100,000. Fellow coaches, I make no apology for reminding you of this most important requirement. *Please* make sure that you are properly insured for cricket coaching. You should also check that your club is properly covered. The NCA or ACC will help you, I am sure, and the cost is small.

DIET

Compared to most other sportsmen, cricketers over the years have hardly been noted for their attention to diet. It is not unknown for fast bowlers to have charged their batteries with a few pints of beer and a large steak before bowling. Nothing could be worse; no wonder their pace went down rather than up!

These days, I am glad to say, players are more conscious of their intake, but, in general, diet still takes second place to physical training, even if one does help

the other. Weight control is vital for long-term success in sport, but the best advice I can give on this subject is to read *Diet in Sport* by Wilf Paish.

FITNESS

Fitness training for individual sports is increasingly becoming a highly specialised field in itself, and in being so has much to offer cricket at all levels of performance. It is important, therefore, for coaches to continually stress what a great benefit qualified fitness training can be towards improving performance. One has only to consider how one or two of the obvious components of physical fitness can have a spectacular effect on a player's success to realise the urgent need for everyone in cricket to recognise the untapped potential of our players. Strength, speed and endurance, for example, can be developed and improved by any player following a well-designed fitness programme. Little imagination is needed to conceive the possibilities of a number of young players hitting the ball like Ian Botham or Viv Richards or bowling with the speed and endurance of Malcolm Marshall. It is not 'pie in the sky' but a very real possibility if it is only recognised by those who are in a position to take action.

In the general training of a cricketer, however, it is unlikely that fitness training specialists will be involved. The job will invariably fall on the capable shoulders of the coach. It is obvious, therefore, that the more knowledge and training expertise the coach has, the better he is able to do the job of coaching, as proper fitness training schedules will need to be integrated into the overall training of any

Fig 89 Training – the normal run-up will seem easy after this.

player seriously wishing to improve his game.

Cricket coaches with ambition should be prepared to attend the special courses that are available (possibly through the National Coaching Foundation) to improve their fitness training capabilities. There are also a number of books that have been written on the subject. The one I like which will be very useful to any cricket coach is *Fitness for Sport* by Rex Hazeldine. Rex is a very capable cricket coach in his own right and this shows in his writing.

'IT'S ALL IN THE MIND'

How many times have we heard this banal comment, true though it is to some extent? Finding an answer to questions of the mind would, indeed, be something very special to accomplish, and to try very hard is an integral part of the coach's job. This does not necessarily involve prying into the thoughts of players, but simply becoming aware of their problems and whether or not the individual is in a good state of mind to play the game.

Kindness, compassion, firmness in decisions, technical and even psychological knowledge are all part of a coach's make-up that can help a player relax and

119

perform to maximum ability when it counts. The acquiring of the skills, the developing of the feelings needed to cope with the responsibilities of the true coach are not an overnight process, but come through experience gained the hard way and by recognising the art and science of coaching as the study of a lifetime.

Motivation of individuals and teams can take many forms. Some, the bullies of coaching, have achieved limited success by fear, but I cannot imagine that this is a worthwhile success. Others motivate by cleverly setting the right goals for individuals and teams. There are a few coaches blessed with the personality to motivate naturally, but these are few and far between. Most of us have to work at it.

The varying emotions of players can be understood by those coaches who simply take a lot of trouble to try to understand, and in their understanding are able to motivate through the respect that their efforts have earned. True respect can come no other way – it must be earned. Stimulation and interest are words that come to mind when thinking of motivation, and time spent considering their possibilities in harness will do a coach no harm; neither does the independent study of sports psychology.

Of all the successful people in sport, none have impressed me more than the former England and Middlesex Captain, Mike Brearley. His ability as a motivator is unsurpassed in my experience, and to read his book, *The Art of Captaincy*, is, in itself, an education in the subject. I should very much like to have played under Mike's captaincy; I am sure he would have lifted my performance by a considerable margin – the inspiration of confidence in the man, if you like.

RELAXATION

There are several ways of helping a player to perform better, but whatever tactic, procedure or technique is used, all must stem from the player being free from tension. The following relaxation procedure may be useful for players and coaches.

PREPARATION

Sit in a comfortable chair or, better still, lie down. Choose a quiet, warm room, when you are not too tired and where you will not be interrupted.

If you are sitting, take off your shoes, uncross your legs and rest your arms along the arms of the chair. If you are lying down, lie on your back, with your arms at your sides.

Close your eyes and be aware of your body: notice how you are breathing and where the muscular tensions in your body are. Make sure you are comfortable.

BREATHING

Start to breathe slowly and deeply, expanding your abdomen as you breathe *in*, then raising your rib-cage to let more air in, till your lungs are filled right to the top. Hold your breath for a couple of seconds and then breathe *out* slowly, allowing your rib-cage and stomach to relax, and empty your lungs completely.

Do not strain, with practice it will become much easier.

Maintain this slow, deep rhythmic breathing throughout your relaxation session.

Fig 90 Team spirit exemplified. Somehow this photograph
shows why Mike Brearley was a great captain.

RELAXATION

After you have got your breathing pattern established, start the following sequence:

1. Curl your toes hard and press your feet down. Tense up on an *in* breath, hold your breath for ten seconds while you keep your muscles tense, then relax and breathe *out* at the same time.

2. Now press your heels down and bend your feet up. Tense up on an *in* breath, hold your breath for ten seconds; relax on an *out* breath.

3. Now tense your calf muscles. Tense up on an *in* breath, hold for ten seconds; relax on an *out* breath.

4. Now tense your thigh muscles, straightening your knees and making your legs stiff. Tense up on an *in* breath; hold for ten seconds; relax on an *out* breath.

5. Now make your buttocks tight. Tense up on an *in* breath; hold for ten seconds; relax on an *out* breath.

6. Now tense your stomach as if to receive a punch. Tense up on an *in* breath; hold for ten seconds; relax on an *out* breath.

7. Now bend your elbows and tense the muscles of your arms. Tense up on an *in* breath; hold for ten seconds; relax on an *out* breath.

8. Now hunch your shoulders and press

121

your head back into the cushion. Tense up on an *in* breath; hold for ten seconds; relax on an *out* breath.

9. Now clench your jaws, frown and screw up your eyes really tight. Tense up on an *in* breath; hold for ten seconds; relax on an *out* breath.

10. Now tense all your muscles together. Tense up on an *in* breath; hold for ten seconds; relax on an *out* breath.

Remember to breathe deeply and be aware, when you relax, of the feeling of physical well-being and heaviness spreading through your body.

After you have completed the sequence from 1 to 10, still breathing slowly and deeply, imagine a white rose on a black background. Try to 'see' the rose as clearly as possible, concentrating your attention on it for thirty seconds. Do *not* hold your breath during this time; continue to breathe as you have been doing. *Repeat* this process, this time thinking of a simple spring scene; for example, a carpet of bluebells set amongst beautiful trees, beside a swiftly flowing stream. Give yourself the instruction that when you open your eyes, you will be perfectly relaxed, but alert. Count to three and then open your eyes.

When you have become familiar with this technique, if you want to relax at any time when you only have a few minutes do the sequence in shortened form, leaving out some muscle groups but always working from your feet upwards. For example, you might do numbers 1, 4, 6, 8 and 10, if you do not have time to do the complete sequence.

The subject of mental training for athletes is very well covered in the fascinating book *Sporting Body – Sporting Mind* by John Syer and Christopher Conolly.

THE NON-TURF PITCH

The very name 'non-turf pitch' can be off-putting. 'Non' seems very negative, and it just does not sound like a cricket term. 'Wicket' is the usual cricketers' description of the cricket playing surface. But non-turf pitch or wicket is a term cricketers should get used to, as without question non-turf pitches hold the answer to the future development of our great game.

I say this simply because the future of the game, as every coach knows, relies on young cricketers learning to play on a surface that will give them enjoyment in playing. Increasingly the turf pitches on which our youngsters are learning the game give anything but enjoyment and on many grounds are just dangerous. Consistent and not unreasonable bounce of the ball, either high or low, develops the skills of both batsman and bowler. As skill develops so does interest and enjoyment.

If the majority rather than the minority of our recreational cricket, particularly at junior level, was played on non-turf pitches, in my opinion cricket would be a better game. In every one of the countless matches that are played every summer, the quality of the playing surface and, in fact, the outfield to a great extent determines the quality and potential enjoyment of the game. Perhaps these notes will instil in coaches a realisation of the situation and more importantly the will to do something about it. If you really are a true coach you will have no alternative.

Let me define a little more clearly what a good pitch or wicket is. It is a true playing surface, with an even and reasonable bounce: reasonable being between three-quarters and just over stump height

Fig 91 Non-turf pitches hold the answer to the future
development of cricket.

from a pace bowler's good length. An
even bounce gives the batsman the confidence to play strokes. Too low a
bounce restricts stroke-making and tends
to produce a negative game. Too high a
bounce from a good length can be dan-

gerous and not at all in the best interests
of the game.

A good wicket should also not react *too*
much on the ball in terms of spin or seam.
That is, considerable spin should need to
be applied by the bowler to produce any

deviations off the wicket. This principle, if fully appreciated, could have the effect of producing more leg break bowling, always a very attractive bowling variation in cricket.

Another feature of a good wicket in my opinion, is that it should not assist the seam bowler on anything but the isolated occasion. This is not meant to decry the bowler who has the ability to deliberately and consistently land the ball on the seam, it is simply to ensure that the ball itself when it does land on the seam does not deviate in an unpredictable manner. There is the possibility that even the world's best batsmen can be dismissed almost by accident when the 'phantom' seamer, as he is known, just happens to hit the seam and bowl the unplayable delivery. Unplayable deliveries should be by design rather than by accident. That is how great bowlers are made.

Even these few words indicate the vital importance of the playing surface in cricket. This dialogue is not meant to be a treatise on groundsmanship, but it is intended to enlist the coach's aid in producing good wickets generally and introducing, where it may not be known, the possibilities of the non-turf pitch.

Composition of the Non-turf Pitch

Different materials are used, but in general it can be said that a non-turf pitch consists of a mat ranging from a quarter to half an inch thick, laid flat on a prepared and firm base. The base can be solid in the form of concrete or porous in some combination of sand, soil, aggregate and so on.

All the well-known surfaces (mats) sold to any degree in the United King-dom are satisfactory, providing they are laid on the appropriate base and finished to a good standard.

In general, synthetic turf is used on a hard porous base, whilst a PVC type mat is laid on a concrete base. Carpet-type materials are suitable when laid on either porous or concrete bases.

Selection of Base and Surface

The selection of the type of base and surface is dependent on a number of factors, the most important being:

1. The age of the players who will use the pitch.
2. Whether a changeable pitch is desirable (that is, a pitch that changes according to climatic conditions).
3. Finance available for the installation.
4. Is it possible to give the pitch regular attention?
5. The location of the pitch; in school, club, park and so on, and whether it is intended for match play or practice.

It is essential to:

1. Identify the type of pitch required.
2. Select the most appropriate base.
3. Select the most suitable surface to meet the needs of the standard of cricket played.

I recommend those interested in the non-turf wicket to contact the National Cricket Association for information on suppliers and installers.

BALLS

I have often thought that the subject of balls, particularly cricket balls, deserves a lot more attention from coaches and cricket in general than it has ever been given. What an intriguing historical book could be written by some enterprising author! What an interesting project for an enthusiastic researcher! However, let us concentrate on cricket balls and coaching and in this context I make a plea to coaches to give some serious thought to the importance of the ball in cricket.

We often hear of both the good and bad effects of the game's various ingredients. The pitch seems to be the biggest villain, followed by the outfield and sometimes the light, but these influences are very often a product of the environment on the day. Bats, probably cricket's most talked about piece of equipment, have an important influence on the game at various levels in both performance and cost. In fact, one of cricket's most annoying occurrences stems from the purchase of an expensive bat one week, only to have it broken the following week by some cheap, poor quality ball. Never think that using cheap 'bargain' balls is sound economics, it isn't. One reason why coaches should become 'experts' in equipment is so that they can advise users on how a good balance of performance and cost may be obtained – value for money if you like!

Some cricket balls are praised for the size of the seam on the ball, as though this makes for a better ball somehow. Invariably it does not, as more often than not a high seam is a product of a 'hard' ball which can cause nothing but trouble, not only in damage but also to batsmen. A high seam can also be responsible for unpredictable bounce and excessive lateral movement off the pitch, neither of which help cricket at all. Many is the time I have seen the most ordinary bowlers

look like world beaters, when using poor quality balls with a pronounced seam. No wonder batsmen lose confidence in practice, when obviously little effective coaching or teaching can take place.

Allied to the technical problems of playing with unsuitable balls is the question of cost. It seems that before long the very best Test match balls could cost over £50 each. Even the cost of the normal club ball can be exorbitant. Fortunately, the manufacturers recognise the problem and are trying to do something about it. Administrators throughout the game also recognise that adjustments need to be made and that, if necessary, cricket can be played very satisfactorily with balls made of materials other than the traditional. This idea applies very much to practice and junior matches at schools and clubs. I expect much progress to be made in this field in the future, as those responsible begin to pay as much attention to the ball as they do the other fascinating variables of cricket.

Finally there is another aspect of ball knowledge that can add to the coaching scene. That is, the possible variations in play that can be offered to a batsman on a standard indoor surface by using a variety of balls. For example, the soft rubber ball will produce the effect of a slow 'stopping' wicket, which takes spin. Alternatively a hard plastic ball will give a very fast bounce from the wicket with little lateral deviation. Balls of different colours can be utilised effectively for practice and coaching. I have found the 'two tone' ball, half white half red on either side of the seam, a great benefit when coaching bowling, especially when using video. Remember also when coaching young bowlers how important it can be to use the junior $4\frac{3}{4}$oz ball. Small

Fig 92   A bowling machine in use, with one of Dorset's lady
coaches batting.

hands need to grip the ball properly if they are to learn the important skills at an early age.

COACHING EQUIPMENT

There is such a variety of equipment to choose from these days, that I shall settle for listing items that you may consider necessary, depending upon your involvement, and which can serve as a reminder.

1. Video tape recording system (including a tripod).
2. 35mm colour slides used with audio/visual system.
3. 16mm film projector and films.
4. 35mm SLR camera system, preferably with motor drive for black and white sequence photography.
5. Overhead projector for lectures, talks and so on.
6. Blackboard and chalk.
7. Cassette tape recorder.
8. Bowling machine.
9. Binoculars.
10. Magnifying glass/light box to view photographs and slides.
11. Several types of balls.
12. Bats and bat shapes.
13. Protective equipment as necessary.
14. Coaching literature.

Group Coaching Inventory

For thirty or more junior players

Bats – six.
Bat shapes – fourteen.
Balls, tennis – twenty-four to forty,
  leather – ten,
  plastic/rubber – ten,
  airflow – ten.

Wickets (portable) – six or eight sets of three.
Pads – six pairs.
Wicket-keeping gloves (with inners) – three pairs.
Batting gloves – six pairs.
Protectors – five.
Skittles or flags – twelve.
Marker boards – eight.
Pencils – eight.
Work cards – various.
Wrist/stop-watches as required.
Scoresheets.
Chalk.
Coloured adhesive tape.
Measuring tape.
String.
Ball boxes.
Batting boards (four feet square for outdoors).
Bowling targets.
Trolley to contain above.

COACH ASSESSMENT

For those who are responsible for coaching performance, whether it be the leader of a group of coaches or a single coach, nothing but good can come from a realistic and qualified assessment of overall coaching performance. Even a self-assessment does no harm. In fact, coach assessment or evaluation is an essential to the future of cricket coaching if it is to achieve credibility in the game at large.

The coach assessment charts (shown in Fig 93) define one method of achieving some consistency in coach assessment. Depending upon the coach's brief, variations can be introduced providing the principles are adhered to.

Planning – Preparation – Organisation	A	B	C	D	E
Was the session/course well constructed? Was the coaching material suitable? Was there enough material? Were the objectives made clear? Was the equipment well organised? Was the group/course well organised? Was a sound monitoring system completed? Was there efficient use of the time available? Were safety considerations adequate?					
Course/Session: Comment:	Date: Coach:				

Coaching Techniques and Communication	A	B	C	D	E
Were instructions given clearly, concisely and audibly? Were the teaching/coaching points made effectively? Were good demonstrations given? Was the language and amount of verbalisation appropriate? Did the coach show ability to spot faults? Did the coach use appropriate questioning? Did the coach show bias in any way? Did the coach appear to have an open mind? Did the coach motivate the individual/group?					
Course/Session: Comment:	Date: Coach:				

A – Excellent   B – Good   C – Average   D – Below Average   E – Unsatisfactory

Fig 93   Coach assessment charts.

12 Summary

In reading this study of cricket coaching, I hope you commenced at the very beginning with the Introduction. If so, I also hope that you have successfully linked the various chapters to give you a solid base and even a set of options in your future coaching and administration of cricket.

As you will have realised fairly quickly, whilst this book presents different aspects of the coach's work, a sound knowledge of the game's skills are just as essential as the attitudes you apply to the job as a whole. It is one thing reading about a subject, but quite another putting into practice what you read; unless you do, however, the immense amount of time and effort involved will have been wasted, or at least not really worthwhile. Both you and I will have failed to some degree and if this should be the case it is for me to apologise. Alternatively, we may have been successful and as a result of our combined efforts someone, somewhere will have benefited, as will cricket itself.

I now put forward a series of questions for *you* to answer with 'yes' or 'no'. If just some of your 'yes' answers have come with the help of the preceding pages or from *The Skills of Cricket* our time has not been wasted; in which case 'many thanks'.

QUESTIONS FOR COACHES

1. Can you give forty children under fourteen years of age an enjoyable two or three hours, whilst at the same time teaching them *all* at least one of the skills of cricket? A cricket ground or large sports hall will be available, plenty of equipment and even one or two helpers.
2. Four sixteen year old boys (two batsmen, two bowlers) in the local cricket club are having a miserable season – last season they were all considered to have outstanding promise. Do you think you can help them to sort out their problems and recover their form?
3. The local cricket club wants to form a junior section. Can you help?
4. You have been asked to manage the county under sixteen squad on their tour of the south of England; can you tackle the job?
5. The county cricket club needs a Youth Development Officer to be responsible for the organisation of its development programme. This requires working with the county association and its coaches. Would you give it a try?
6. The local junior school needs someone to give basic instruction to a couple of its teachers and half a dozen others from local schools on how to introduce cricket into the schools locally and set up a junior league. Can you do it?
7. Can you explain the LBW law?
8. Can you explain the no-ball law?
9. Could you give a talk on group coaching?
10. Could you demonstrate the principles of group coaching?
11. Could you organise an evening net coaching session for under sixteens at

your local club?

12. Given the space on a sports field, together with suitable equipment and help, could you set up three separate cricket games for players under thirteen years of age, none of which must be eleven-a-side?

13. Could you complete a simple skill analysis form for eighteen year old batsmen/bowlers that may be useful to another coach?

14. Could you make recommendations to a school or club on what facilities and equipment they may need for playing junior cricket?

15. Could you design a two or three day holiday cricket coaching course for your county for up to thirty or thirty-five children, aged approximately fourteen years, providing facilities, overnight accommodation and meals?

16. Do you recognise that satisfactory cricket equipment and facilities for all levels of play and age groups need not be too expensive. That is, do you know what is needed in terms of value for money?

17. Do you recognise that safety is a prime responsibility in coaching?

18. Do you accept the outstanding need for proper monitoring of players by coaches?

19. Do coaches need to be assessed periodically?

20. Could you identify the majority of common faults in batting and bowling?

21. Could you give a talk on how to teach bowling?

22. Could you identify the key positions in the bowling action?

23. Do you know the basic principles of straight bat play?

24. You need £500 to develop junior cricket in your area. You have one or two kindred spirits from flourishing clubs to support you. Do you think that you could raise the money and ensure that it is properly used?

25. If you have read this far, is there any need to ask you if you enjoy coaching young cricketers? (There has to be *one* 'no' at least!)

Bibliography

The following are publications linked to this book which will be useful to cricket coaches.

The Art of Captaincy, Mike Brearley (Hodder & Stoughton)

Cricket Umpiring and Scoring, Tom Smith (J. M. Dent & Sons)

Diet in Sport, Wilf Paish (A & C Black)

First Aid Manual (Royal Life Saving Society/St John Ambulance Association)

Fitness for Sport, Rex Hazeldine (The Crowood Press)

MCC Coaching Book (Heinemann)

The Skills of Cricket, Keith Andrew (The Crowood Press)

Sporting Body – Sporting Mind, Syer and Connolly (Cambridge)

'Test' Cricket in Clubs and Schools (National Cricket Association)

The National Coaching Scheme (National Cricket Association)

Index

Crowood Sports Books

Badminton – The Skills of the Game   Peter Roper
Basketball – The Skills of the Game   Paul Stimpson
Canoeing – Skills and Techniques   Neil Shave
* The Skills of Cricket   Keith Andrew
Fitness for Sport   Rex Hazeldine
* Golf – The Skills of the Game   John Stirling
Hockey – The Skills of the Game   John Cadman
Coaching Hockey   David Whitaker
Judo – Skills and Techniques   Tony Reay
Jumping   Malcolm Arnold
Rugby Union – The Skills of the Game   Barrie Corless
Skiing – Developing Your Skill   John Shedden
Sprinting and Hurdling   Peter Warden
Squash – The Skills of the Game   Ian McKenzie
Swimming   John Verrier
Table Tennis – The Skills of the Game   Gordon Steggall
Volleyball – The Skills of the Game   Keith Nicholls

* Also available in paperback

Further details of titles available or in preparation
can be obtained from the publishers.